Osaka Insider

A Travel Guide for Osaka Prefecture

D1602357

Patrick Mackey

Guidebook maps: http://osakainsider.wordpress.com/guidebook-maps

Osaka Insider blog: http://osakainsider.wordpress.com

Finding Fukuoka blog: http://findingfukuoka.wordpress.com

Translation services: http://fukuokatranslation.wordpress.com

翻訳サービス: http://fukuokahonyaku.wordpress.com

ISBN-13: 978-1466419971

ISBN-10: 1466419970

Printed in the United States of America.

For my brother Chris.

You taught me to thrive amidst adversity and fear nothing.

Contents

Essays

Maps and Reference

Acknowledgments

Even though I took on this project alone, there is almost nothing in life that can be accomplished without the support of others, and I would like to acknowledge a few of the many people helped me directly and indirectly with this book. First is my wife Yoko, who gave me the encouragement and support I needed. My sister and mom also deserve special thanks for helping with proofreading. The staff at Japanese Guest Houses and Japan Roads gave me my first experience working in the travel industry and set me on the path that led to the writing of this book. My extremely talented co-workers at GK Associates (Osaka) gave me some tough lessons and invaluable experience in writing and editing, and also pushed me to improve my Japanese skills. I also want to give a special thanks to all the readers of my *Osaka Insider* blog, whose kind and insightful comments encouraged me to keep writing—without loyal readers like you, this book never would have happened. And of course, I want to give a special thanks to everyone who believed in and encouraged me along the way.

What Makes This Guidebook Unique

Osaka is, without a doubt, one of the most interesting, unique, and welcoming places in Japan, not to mention extremely important in terms of culture and history. But because of its location in the Kansai region, surrounded by Kyoto, Nara, Himeji, and other major tourist destinations, it often gets left behind, judged to be a polluted, big-city commercial center and nothing more. Many tourists visit Osaka Castle, shop a bit in Umeda, perhaps stop over at Universal Studios Japan, and then leave Osaka without ever knowing a thing about it. It's as if they visited Osaka with their eyes closed.

As anyone familiar with the workings of the travel industry knows, not all companies writing travel books on destinations around the world are reliable. In fact, it is because they are such large-scale companies that they do not always produce adequate guidebooks, and sometimes the researchers and writers in charge of covering Japan are not properly educated on its culture and language. Some go as far as taking information from tourist information offices and reproducing it in the target audience's language, without actually setting foot in most of places. Predictably, Osaka is poorly represented as a result—if represented at all. Such sightseeing guides promote things people have already decided to see rather than suggesting anything new that may change people's perspectives, with a primary goal of making money (even if this lowers the depth and quality of the reader's trip).

The government of Osaka City has made tremendous efforts in recent times to bring in more tourists, and these efforts have paid off well. But the challenge faced by Osaka's municipal and prefectural governments—which, until now, have provided the best sources of information in English—is that they are obligated to promote everything without discernment when it comes to tourism, even if some of the places they mention really aren't worth visiting. This sometimes results in an excessively large collection of data that an inexperienced tourist cannot hope to navigate. Additionally, government organizations have difficulty grasping the type of sightseeing spots that visitors from abroad are interested in seeing, instead providing translations of sightseeing information originally intended for Japanese tourists.

Of course there are a number of guides in Japanese that focus on Osaka in great detail, and some of them are quite good. But there has never been anything of that quality available in English.

Travel guides, government-created websites and tourism materials, and other such sources of information have been invaluable resources for me and helped form the foundations of my knowledge on Osaka. But I wanted do things differently. I have visited every single destination and every single shop listed in this book, and evaluated each one based on my knowledge and experience. There are no personal politics involved, no corporate or bureaucratic structure to stop me from saying the things I have to say or the things you need to know. Essentially, you are getting a private tour from me every time you use this book.

I also intend to do something many Japanese guidebooks don't do: focus not just on Osaka City, but on Osaka Prefecture as whole. Many of the most interesting sights are available outside of the city, in the more rural parts of a prefecture that has an overwhelmingly urban image.

My goal is to help you fall in love with Osaka as I did, and to make sure you have an unforgettable visit. I have tried to be as unbiased as possible and take into consideration the preferences and interests of a wide range of travelers. The information within can be used by foreign nationals living in Japan as well as tourists from abroad.

In Osaka, there is so much waiting to be found below the surface. It is a place that deserves at least one detailed English-language guidebook.

About Me

I was born and raised in Oregon (USA) and graduated from University of Oregon *cum laude* in 2006 with a triple major in Japanese, Asian studies, and history, having spent a term studying at Waseda University in Tokyo along the way. After graduation, I immediately came to Japan, living in Toyama for a short time before moving to Osaka. It wasn't long before I became infatuated with the city, and after thoroughly exploring every street and alley, I started to travel around the rest of the prefecture as well, not to mention the rest of Kansai.

My first job in Kansai was at a small travel agency in Kawanishi (Hyogo Prefecture), where I designed and helped coordinate tours while assisting guests from overseas in making reservations at traditional Japanese lodging places (*ryokan, minshuku, shukubo,* etc.). After that I entered a translation company in Tenmabashi (Osaka City) and gained a wealth of valuable experience as the in-house editor/translator. I also passed the level 2 and then level 1 Japanese Language Proficiency Examinations (JLPT) during this time—equivalent to levels N3–N1 in the newer JLPT system—and continued to study Japanese language and Japanese history in my free time while taking advantage of every chance I could get to travel around Japan. I began writing my *Osaka Insider* blog (http://osakainsider.wordpress.com) during my time as an in-house editor/translator, and watched as it became a popular

English-language resource for information on Osaka and developed a moderate sized and diverse group of loyal readers.

I also began compiling sightseeing information that would become the basis for this book, visiting each and every destination in person to give it a fair rating and to decide if it was really worth recommending to others. In early 2011, I moved to Fukuoka, a lovely city in Kyushu, and began writing my next blog, *Finding Fukuoka* (http://findingfukuoka.wordpress.com), while put-ting this guidebook together and working as a freelance translator and editor (http://fukuokatranslation.wordpress.com).

I plan to continue promoting my Japanese "hometown" of Osaka while exploring my new home in Fukuoka. I hope all the hard work I put into this guidebook will be of use to you, and most of all, I hope you will enjoy your time in Osaka as much as I did.

Osaka in Photographs

The following are photographs of a few of the destinations listed in this guidebook. Page numbers for relevant information are provided next to each photograph. As with others throughout this guidebook, all photographs were taken by the author.

Osaka Castle (p. 94) with Osaka Business Park (p. 101) partially visible in the background.

Above: Umeda district (p. 71). Below: Kokaido (Osaka Central Public Hall) on the riverine island of Nakanoshima (p. 81).

Above: The Namba Parks shopping center (p. 53). Below: Tower of the Sun (*Taiyo no To*) in Banpaku Memorial Park (p. 150).

Above: Dotombori, Namba (p. 49). Below: Sojiji Temple (p. 153).

Above: Sumiyoshi Grand Shrine (p. 124). Below: "Love Foxes" at Tamatsukuri Inari Shrine (p. 107).

Above: Festival boats on the Okawa River during the Tenjin Matsuri festival (p. 177). Below: An Aqua Bus sightseeing boat (p. 51) near Tenmabashi (p. 87).

Above: Tenjinbashisuji Shopping Arcade (p. 91). Below: Naniwa Yasaka Shrine (p. 55).

Tondabayashi Jinaimachi Temple Town (p. 131): Walking the streets (above) and touring an old residence (below).

Above: Tsutenkaku ("Tower to the Heavens") and the Shinsekai district (p. 103). Below: Eifukuji Temple (Prince Shotoku's Mausoleum) (p. 129).

Above: Open-Air Museum of Old Japanese Farmhouses (p. 148). Below: Umeda Sky Building (p. 72).

Above: Ikoma Building in Kitahama (pp. 86, 206). Below: Old Sakai Lighthouse (p. 139).

Above: Spring cherry blossoms at the Osaka Mint (p. 176). Below: Takidani Fudo Myo-oji Temple (p. 130).

Above: Hagi-no-tera Toko-in Temple (p. 150). Below: A fresh food market in Tsuruhashi (p. 105).

Above: People walking circles around two stones while praying at Ishikiri-Tsurugiya Shrine (p. 155). Below: Osaka branch of the Bank of Japan on Nakanoshima (pp. 81, 202).

Above: Yodogawa Lagoons / Shirokita Park (p. 113). Below: Kishiwada Castle (p. 142).

Above: Garden at Fujita-tei Remains Park and Museum (p. 98). Below: Hozanji Temple on Mount Ikoma (p. 157).

Orientation and Useful Information

Location and Climate

Osaka City has a population of about 2.7 million, with a greater metropolitan area population of about 20 million. It has the largest daytime and nighttime population difference among Japan's cities, with a daytime population increase of about 40%[1] due to people commuting in for work—hence the incredibly efficient transportation network. It is located on the Kinki Plain, and faces Osaka Bay to the west (which borders both the Seto Inland Sea and the Pacific Ocean). Osaka is located at the center of the Kansai region, an area that also includes Hyogo, Wakayama, Nara, Kyoto, Mie and Shiga Prefectures.

The Shinkansen (often known by the Western nickname "bullet train") stops at Shin-Osaka Station, the terminus for both the Sanyo and Tokaido Shinkansen Lines. Services as far as Tokyo are available going east and as far as Kagoshima in southern Kyushu going west. The two main urban centers in Osaka are Umeda and Namba: the area including Umeda, Kitashinchi, Chayamachi, Doyamacho, and sometimes Nakazakicho and Juso are referred to by locals as "Kita" (lit. "North"), and the area including Namba, Soemoncho, Dotombori, Shinsaibashi, Nagahoribashi, Kita-Horie/Minami-Horie, Nipponbashi (including Den Den Town), Yotsubashi and Amemura are referred to as "Minami" (lit. "South"). Kyobashi and Tennoji are also large subcenters, and much of the finance, government and business sectors are located in Osaka Business Park (OBP) and the Honmachi/Kitahama/Tenmabashi areas, as well as the aforementioned centers and subcenters.

---

1 http://www.stat.go.jp/english/data/kokusei/2000/jutsu1/00/01.htm

JR Osaka Station, Hankyu Umeda Station, Hanshin Umeda Station, and three Umeda-area subway stations provide access to Umeda, and Osaka-Namba Station (Kintetsu and Hanshin lines), Nankai Namba Station, JR Namba Station, and three Namba subway stations serve Namba. Kansai International Airport is connected to the city by Nankai and JR rail lines, as well as by bus and expressway. Osaka (Itami) International Airport is a smaller airport used for domestic flights, and it is connected to the city by Hankyu and Osaka Monorail lines, as well as by bus and expressway.

A humid subtropical climate, Osaka has four distinct seasons with mild winters (it usually only snows in the mountains on the edges of the prefecture), very hot and humid summers, and a rainy season that usually lasts from late May or early June until mid-July. Spring and autumn are the most pleasant times to visit, and they are also the times when cherry blossoms bloom and the autumn colors appear, respectively. There are rarely earthquakes in Osaka (which also means tsunamis are also rare), typhoons generally don't come close enough to pose any direct threat, and there are no active volcanoes in or near Osaka that pose any danger.

Osaka History and Culture

Osaka, often overshadowed by Tokyo despite its much more fascinating and unique history, has played many roles in its long history dating back to before the seventh century. It was originally known as Naniwa-kyo (難波京), one of the first imperial capitals of Japan during Emperor Kotoku's reign. The *kanji* characters—originally Chinese characters now used in Japanese—for Naniwa (難波) are now read as Namba, the name of the famous entertainment, shopping and nightlife district in Minami. The city's Naniwa Ward (浪速区) also shows ties to the former capital's name. After the capital moved elsewhere, Naniwa later became the capital again for a brief time in the eighth century under Emperor Shomu. The name Osaka (大坂) is recorded in documents as far back as the fifteenth century, although the *kanji* characters were changed from 大坂 to 大阪 (the latter its modern-day name) because part of the second character in the old name is indirectly associated with the negative meaning of "death."

Shitennoji Temple (see p. 109), located in southern central Osaka and constructed in the sixth century, was the first officially recognized Buddhist Temple in Japan. Buddhist influence had a tight hold over Osaka until Oda Nobunaga, the first of the three great unifiers of Japan who would help end a long period of bloody civil war, used military force to dislodge their power. Under Toyotomi Hideyoshi (r. 1585–1591), the second of the great unifiers, Osaka grew into a great and powerful metropolis, with Hideyoshi's spectacular castle at the center (see p. 94). At that time, it was the largest and most awe-inspiring castle in Japan, and it is still a powerful symbol of the city today. After Hideyoshi died, his son Hideyori was supposed to ascend to the position of Shogun in Hideyoshi's place, but Tokugawa Ieyasu (the third and final unifier) and his allies betrayed those loyal to the Toyotomi and became the new rulers of Japan, ushering in a period of peace and growth and moving the government center out of Kansai to Edo (now Tokyo). However, Hideyori would remain a problem for the Tokugawa regime, as many still rallied around him and his base of power in Osaka; it took many years and two large-scale military campaigns, but the Tokugawa eventually wiped out Toyotomi lineage, and the young Hideyori committed suicide with his mother while the battered Osaka Castle burned around him.

The ascendance of the Tokugawa family ushered in the peaceful Edo Period (1600–1868), a time of new growth and change in Japanese society. Samurai were forced by law to relocate to castle towns, and only one castle town was allowed in each feudal domain (each headed by a *daimyo* lord, who in turn was loyal to the Shogun in the capital of Edo). Osaka was chosen as the main power center in Western Japan for the *bakufu* (the semi-feudal central government headed by the Shogun), and the city grew to become Japan's most important commercial entrepôt where goods were sold and stored, later to be resold or redistributed throughout the country. Unlike other castles towns, the samurai population in Osaka was very small, and its merchant population very large, leading to the reputation of Osaka as a city of commerce and entertainment. It became known as the "City of Water" because of the network of canals crisscrossing the city (boat being the main form of transport around town), and also as the "Merchant's Capital." *Bunraku* puppet theater, one of the most cherished traditional art forms in Japan, became popularized first in Osaka during the Edo Period, and today Osaka is still the cultural center for this art form (see p. 63). Because of its merchant past and emphasis on commerce, Osaka's food is still widely considered to be among the best in Japan (and also some of the most fairly priced)—the phrase *kuidaore*, or "eat until you drop," is often used in descriptions of gourmet culture in Osaka.

The Meiji Restoration in 1868 was a relatively peaceful revolution that established a parliamentary government based on a modern constitution. In a broad sense, the revolution started from Kyushu and Shikoku and moved eastward toward Tokyo, and during that time Osaka was a major rallying point for the rebels rising up against the *bakufu* government ruled by the Tokugawa family. As it has done for most of its history, Osaka was as an important port of trade not only domestically but between Japan other countries as well, and this role grew increasingly important during the modern period as Japan industrialized and modernized at a rapid pace never before seen in world history. Osaka also became an important center for manufacturing in Japan and fueled the economic machine that would make the country a major world power by the start of the twentieth century. At the time, Osakans took pride in the city's newest nickname, the "City of Smoke," which was coined due to pollution in the air generated by concentrations of factories located within and near the city. Many people considered factories and smog to be symbols of "progress" and equality with other great world powers—the basis of a strong country that would not be ruthlessly colonized by Western powers as much of Asia had been.

In 1923, when the Great Kanto Earthquake and ensuing fires completely destroyed the national capital of Tokyo, Osaka replaced it as the administrative center of Japan for a brief time. In 1945, aside from the two atomic bombs dropped on Hiroshima and Nagasaki, 66 other cities in Japan were burned to the ground by allied incendiary bombings that took hundreds of thousands of lives.[2]

---

[2] *Overall Report of Damage Sustained by the Nation During the Pacific War.* Economic Stabilization Agency, Planning Department, Office of the Secretary General, 1949.

Osaka was among the 66 cities decimated, and it had to be almost entirely rebuilt after the war ended.

Following World War II, after order was restored somewhat with assistance from the allied occupation, Japan's economy once again grew, this time at a faster pace than it had during the prewar period. Osaka again became the center of manufacturing in Japan for several decades until factories began moving overseas to other parts of Asia. In recent decades, most factories within city limits have disappeared and the service industry has become the dominant industry in Osaka and Japan as a whole. While Osaka held a reputation for being a dirty and dangerous city during the prewar and early postwar periods, it has undergone a drastic transformation to become one of Japan's most pleasant places to live. It has one of the most thorough and well-planned public transportation networks in the world, and the population of the greater the metropolitan area (including Kobe, Kyoto and other parts of Kansai) has ballooned to about 20 million people. Osaka has the highest ratio of change between daytime and nighttime populations (approximately 40% population increase during the day[3]), which is just one sign of its strong commercial character and the break from its industrial "City of Smoke" past.

Today, Osaka has become a dynamic, forward-moving city, constantly growing and innovating thanks to its people and leaders. Kansai International Airport, built on an artificial island in the bay, has become one of the three major international airports in Japan. Universal Studios Japan was built in Osaka, located conveniently close to the city center, to rival Tokyo Disney Resort.

Culturally, Osaka is known for its food, the frank and welcoming character of its citizens, its comedians (Osaka is the center of Japanese comedy) and other aspects. It has a long-standing rivalry with Tokyo, although Tokyoites seem to spend more time criticizing Osaka (and every other part of Japan) than Osakans, who generally don't judge outsiders with contempt or care much about Tokyo culture. In addition, the baseball rivalry between the Hanshin Tigers of Osaka/Kobe and the Yomiuri Giants of Tokyo, as well as

---

[3] http://www.stat.go.jp/english/data/kokusei/2000/jutsu1/00/01.htm

the soccer rivalry between Gamba Osaka and the Urawa Red Diamonds of Saitama (a Tokyo suburb), are some of the fiercest in Japanese sports.

Osakans are known to be down-to-earth and have pride in their city, but their pride almost never leads to arrogance, and they gladly welcome and accept newcomers. It is also one of Japan's most international cities. In other words, you are sure to make some friends during your visit.

Transportation

Osaka has one of the most comprehensive and efficient public transportation networks in Japan, and it is always expanding. This network not only provides a sound base for a strong economy, it enables travelers and citizens to move around with ease. The following is a basic guide for using the public transportation system in Osaka Prefecture; it is geared mainly toward those who have never spent time in Japan.

■ Ticket Machines and Ticket Gates

Some machines have English user interfaces, but even for machines that don't, usage is straightforward: look at the route map located above or near the machine, put money into the machine, push the appropriate button to buy a ticket for the amount listed on the route map, and take your change if necessary. Some machines don't accept large bills (check near the money slot to see if bills above 1,000 yen are accepted), but coins are always accepted.

If you are riding JR trains and want to buy a limited express or Shinkansen ("bullet train") ticket, use a green ticket machine and choose the English language option before beginning. The machine will guide you through the purchasing process and issue your tickets at the end. You can also enter a ticket office and buy tickets for JR lines (or any other lines) directly from a staff member.

When you go through the ticket gate, put your ticket in and collect it as it comes out the slot at the other end of the gate. When you pass through the ticket gate again at your destination, put the ticket in and leave (it will not be returned to you unless it is a reusable pass). If the ticket gates close and an error message is displayed, it means you probably have not paid the correct amount and need to pay an additional charge before being allowed to exit. In this case, put your ticket in a fare adjustment machine (located near the ticket gates), insert the amount of money shown on the screen, and use the new ticket issued to pass through the ticket gates. You can also talk directly to a staff member (usually they are behind a window near the ticket gates) if you are confused or want to pay in person instead of using the fare adjustment machine.

■ Streetcars and Buses

For streetcars (Hankai lines), enter through the back door and pay by putting your fare into the box next to the driver when you leave. There are change machines next to the fare boxes in the front and back of the car, in case you are not carrying correct change (the Hankai Streetcar Line costs either 200 yen or 290 yen, depending on the distance you are traveling).

Buses work much like streetcars, although fares vary more depending on the distance you travel; however, some buses have a set price. Enter through the back door, take a number from the machine near the entrance (you will show this to the driver when you leave to indicate the fare you owe—there will be no numbers on fixed-fare buses) and exit from the front when you get off. Payment and change machines work the same as with streetcars.

■ Taxis

Calling a taxi in Osaka City is as easy as raising your hand in the air, and when outside of the city you can easily find one at the nearest station or main boulevard. In the more rural parts of the prefecture, you may need to call a taxi company by phone in order to be picked up—you can ask a nearby business owner or train station employee for a number, but you will usually need to use a payphone or mobile phone and speak Japanese. Taxis are not cheap in Japan, but they are convenient. Some taxi drivers speak English, but this is rare, so it is easiest to show the driver one of the Japanese-language destination names/addresses displayed in this guidebook (this usually suffices), or have the address or directions to your destination written out in Japanese beforehand.

■ Rental Bicycles

Rental bicycles are available at many major stations in the suburbs and rural areas. Riding a bicycle is an enjoyable way to move around if you're feeling a bit adventurous, because you have a chance to see all the small streets and shops along the way you might miss by taking a subway, train, bus or taxi. If possible, pick up a sightseeing map (usually available at bicycle rental shops) so that you won't get lost.

■ Train Passes

There are a number of convenient train passes, which can be used for a given number of times or over a given period of time, that will provide you with discounts and take the hassle out of buying a ticket every time you board a train. The following are some of the best passes for Osaka Prefecture:

- JR Rail Pass: Visitors who plan to enter Japan as tourists are eligible to apply for the JR Rail Pass, which is a great deal if you are planning to travel long distances while in Japan using the Shinkansen ("bullet train") multiple times. This pass enables use of all local trains and limited express trains on JR lines, Shinkansen lines (excluding "Nozomi" and "Mizuho" trains), and some JR buses. There are 7-day, 14-day and 21-day passes available. When entering the station, you will need to show your pass to the ticket gate attendant, as it cannot be used in automated ticket gates. The pass must be purchased from abroad, before you come to Japan. If you plan to stay in the Osaka area only, this pass will not be of much use, especially because privately operated lines and subway lines are far more useful than JR lines in the Osaka area. Visit http://www.japan railpass.net for more information.

- Surutto Kansai Pass: This pass enables unlimited travel on buses, subways, and non-JR train lines in the Kansai region, and both 2-day and 3-day passes are available. The easiest way to purchase this pass is to buy it at Osaka (Itami) International Airport or Kansai International Airport, or at tourism information office in Osaka (see p. 38).

- Enjoy Eco Card: This one-day pass is available every day of the week for 800 yen (300 yen for children), and it enables unlimited use of subways and municipal buses for one day. The Nanko Port Town Line / New Tram Line is counted as a subway line.

- Osaka Municipal Subway Multiple Ride Card: The 3,000 yen card gives you 3,300 yen worth of rides on subways (including the Nanko Port Town Line / New Tram Line) and municipal buses. The 1,500 yen card gives you 1,650 yen worth of rides. The card does not expire, so you can use it over as many days as you like.

- Teku Teku 1-Day Ticket: This 600 yen pass enables unlimited use of the two Hankai streetcar lines for one day. Hankai lines primarily provide access between Osaka City (from Ebisucho or Tennoji) and Sakai City (see p. 134).

How to Find Your Way Around (How to Avoid Getting Lost)

Most streets in Japan are unnamed, although most major intersections are labeled with names next to the traffic signals, with large intersections usually shown in both Japanese and roman letters but smaller intersections only in Japanese. The best way to get around is by following landmarks, and often people will draw up makeshift maps marked with convenience stores and the like when explaining directions. When explaining how to get to destinations listed in this guidebook, I have adopted a similar method, giving detailed instructions on how to walk from the station and where to make turns.

The Minami area of central Osaka City is mostly laid out in a straightforward grid pattern that is easy to navigate, but other parts of the city and prefecture are a tangled mess of small roads, boulevards, and expressways. Although you will find maps posted in train stations and around town in central areas, you may still get lost along the way. If you don't have a full area map already, I recommend picking one up at one of the tourist information offices in Osaka City (see next section).

If you do get lost, as often happens to the best of us, you have several options:

- Ask someone living in the area for directions

- Ask at one of the many convenience stores you will come across (they are equipped with detailed neighborhood maps)

- Ask at a *koban* police box (officers there have even more detailed maps than convenience stores do, and they are used to helping people with directions)

- Hail a taxi and ask to be taken to the destination (expensive but convenient)

Of course, many tourists visiting Japan do not speak or read the language. That's why I have included the names of sightseeing spots and shops in both Japanese and English, and have also included the addresses in Japanese, so you can show them to the person you are asking for directions (or the taxi driver). Even if you speak little to no Japanese, this method will get you where you need to go.

While getting lost in a foreign country can be daunting for some, it is also a good chance to discover things you never would have seen otherwise. Japan is a country with very few unsafe places and many kind people who are willing to help strangers, and as long as you keep your wits about you, being lost might even lead to some of your best travel memories.

Other Useful Information

■ Tourist Information Offices

There are tourist information offices in Shin-Osaka Station, Umeda Station / Osaka Station (near the Midosuji exit if you are taking JR),

Namba Station (near exit 24, closest to the Midosuji and Sennichimae Subway Lines, Kintetsu lines, and Hanshin Namba Line), Tennoji Station (closer to the JR station than the subway station or Kintetsu Osaka-Abenobashi Station), Universal-city Station (the station for Universal Studios Japan on the JR Sakurajima Line / Yumesaki Line), and Kansai International Airport (in the international arrivals lobby). You can pick up maps, pamphlets and a wide range of information in various languages, and the staff can answer your questions in English.

■ Money

Japanese paper money comes in denominations of 1,000, 2,000, 5,000 and 10,000 yen (2,000 yen bills are uncommon), and coins come in denominations of 1, 5, 10, 50, 100 and 500 yen. Although credit cards are accepted at most hotels and some high-end restaurants, Japan is largely a cash-based society. It is best to use international ATMs to withdraw money, such as those at the post offices or international banks like Citibank. Traveler's checks are not widely accepted. If you need to change money, the airport is the best place, because it is very hard to find a place to do this otherwise. Carrying large amounts of cash (30,000 yen or more) is common. If you do plan to use a foreign credit card, it is best to inform your credit company that you will be visiting Japan so they won't think that your credit card has been stolen and block your transactions.

■ Dining

Most table manners in Western countries also apply in Japan. Specific manners mainly concern chopstick use: don't point at people with your chopsticks, don't stab food with them, don't take food out of serving dishes with your own chopsticks (unless you use the opposite end of them), don't pass food from your chopsticks to another person's chopsticks, and never stand them point-first in your rice (this gesture has deep ties with death, and is a major faux pas— instead, place your chopsticks sideways over one of your dishes or on the tray, or on top of a chopstick rest when available). At the start of a meal, it is polite to say *itadakimasu* (ee-tah-dah-kee-mahs), and after eating you can end with *gochisosama deshita* (go-chee-so-sah-mah desh-tah). Some non-Japanese put soy sauce on their white rice for flavoring, but this is considered strange in Japan (a bowl of white rice is usually eaten by itself). With small dishes, it is common practice to pick up the dish with one hand and bring it closer to your mouth when eating, and with dishes containing broth (ramen, *udon*, etc.), it is acceptable to pick up your dish and drink the broth. Do not leave tips at restaurants (or hotels)—this custom does not exist in Japan, and it will put the staff in an awkward position because they will resist taking your money and feel strongly inclined to return it to you. Payment for meals at restaurants usually takes place at the register rather than the table.

■ Crime

The crime rate in Japan is astoundingly low, and there are few parts of town you need to avoid. The few parts of Osaka that might be considered dangerous are areas you will most likely never visit. Obviously, women should take more care than men when walking alone at night or riding crowded trains, and all travelers should use the same common sense they would use at home and avoid trusting suspicious people. However, carrying large amounts of cash is common in Japan, and pickpocketing almost never occurs.

■ Barrier-Free Facilities (Wheelchair Accessibility)

Accessibility for wheelchair users and others who have difficulty using stairs is increasingly available in Osaka, and almost every station is equipped with elevators. Not every sightseeing destination is fully equipped (particularly temples and shrines), but most of the major ones are (even Osaka Castle). For information on accessibility at specific sightseeing spots, refer to the "Accessible Japan" website (in English) at http://www.tesco-premium.co.jp/aj/index.htm.

■ How to Visit Shinto Shrines and Buddhist Temples

Shinto is the native religion of Japan, and it involves worship of numerous deities (*kami*) who are believed to reside in trees, water, rocks, mountains and other parts of nature. Buddhism, on the other hand, was passed on first through India, then China and Korea before coming to Japan in the sixth century. The religion is based on the teachings of Gautama Siddhartha, usually called Shaka in Japanese and more widely known as the Buddha. Shinto and Buddhism harmoniously coexist in Japan today, and both have had great cultural influence on the other (this can be seen by the common mixing of architectural styles and enshrinement of figures from both religions in the same place).

When you enter the grounds of a Shinto shrine, first wash your hands and mouth at the basin beyond the *torii* entrance gate(s): (1) Take water from the basin using one of the ladles and pour it on one hand, then the other; (2) Pour some water into a cupped hand (usually the left), rinse your mouth with the water, and spit the water into the area below the basin (usually another basin or rocks); (3) Rinse the hand you drank out of again; and (4) Fill the ladle again and point it upward with the cup portion on top so that water pours down over the handle, cleansing it. If you want to pay your respects to the deities at the actual shrine, which is not required but not discouraged, throw a coin into the offering box (a 10-yen coin or higher is common), bow deeply from the waist twice, clap your hands twice, bow deeply once again, stand silently with your hands folded flat out in front of you for a few seconds (you may pray silently if you wish), then bow one last time before leaving. If there is a gong or bell, you may ring that before paying your respects (it has the same function of getting the deities' attention that clapping one's hands does). If you do pray at a shrine, do so silently.

At a Buddhist temple, you simply throw a coin, fold your hands flat out in front of you, and pay your respects silently (you usually bow before and after). People do not clap, ring bells, or do other such things at Buddhist temples, although you may occasionally see Japanese visitors do so mistakenly. Some temples have large incense burners: the smoke is said to have special powers such as healing and increasing intelligence, and you can waft some of the smoke over your body using your hands if you wish.

If you are not sure whether you are at a Buddhist temple or a Shinto shrine, the easiest method of confirmation is to check whether it is listed as a temple (Buddhism) or shrine (Shinto) in this guidebook. Generally, if the Japanese version of the name ends in *ji, tera, dera* or *in* in Japanese, it is a Buddhist temple, and if it ends in *jingu, jinja, gu* or *taisha*, it is a Shinto shrine.

Although photography is usually permitted at shrines and temples, you should not take pictures of enshrined objects, especially if there is a sign prohibiting photography. At temples or shrines where entrance into the buildings themselves is permitted, photography is almost always prohibited inside the buildings. And if you do take pictures of historic objects, which are also valuable works of art, turn off your flash because it may cause damage (and it will make you look extremely inconsiderate). Many of Japan's national treasures are stored in temples rather than museums, so you should use the same common sense about photography that you would in a national museum.

I have included shrine/temple hours in the sightseeing sections whenever such information was available. Most shrine and temple facilities are open from 8:00 or 9:00 AM to 4:00 or 5:00 PM, with the shrine gates often being opened earlier (and sometimes later) than the facilities inside for the convenience of worshippers.

Online Resources

The following online resources are useful for visitors to Japan, especially those who carry a portable device or computer with Internet access during their travels:

- *Osaka Insider* (http://osakainsider.wordpress.com): My weblog, featuring sightseeing and living information for Osaka and Kansai. Ramen and bar guides for central Osaka are also available here.

- Osaka-Info (http://www.osaka-info.jp/en): A municipal government sightseeing page. Not every recommendation is good, but it has more information on Osaka sightseeing than any other site I have found.

- Brand-New Osaka (http://www.pref.osaka.jp/en/attraction/visit /index.html): the Osaka Prefectural government's sightseeing page.

- Osaka Municipal Transportation Bureau (http://www.kotsu.city.osaka.jp/foreign/english): The operator of subways and buses in Osaka City. Includes route maps.

- Japan National Tourism Organization: (http://www.jnto.go.jp/eng): Japan's national tourism promotion site, with an abundance of information about travel and sightseeing all over Japan.

- Japan-Guide.com (http://www.japan-guide.com): A popular, considerably thorough site that covers sightseeing and many other topics on Japan in general. Great for general information, as well as for posting any questions you may have (in the forums).

- Accessible Japan (http://www.tesco-premium.co.jp/aj/index.htm): A travel guide for wheelchair users and others who may have trouble using stairs, etc.

- Hyperdia (http://www.hyperdia.com/en): A site where you can look up detailed and accurate departure times, travel times, and fares for every train line in the country. This is especially useful when planning your itinerary.

- Kansai-area railway network access guide (http://www.osaka-info.jp/en/access/info_train.html): Outlines access between Osaka and common destinations, including access to and from airports.

- Wikitravel (http://wikitravel.org): A contributor-based collaborative travel guide similar in structure to Wikipedia. There is plenty of good sightseeing information on this site, particularly related to restaurant and bar recommendations and affordable lodging options.

Emergency Phone Numbers

The following are numbers you can call in case of emergency (the first two can be dialed for free using a public phone):

- Fire or medical emergency: 119
- Police: 110

- Japan Helpline (24-hour general and emergency assistance in numerous languages): 05-7000-0911
- American Consulate in Osaka: 06-6315-5900
- American Embassy in Tokyo: 03-3224-5000
- Australian Consulate in Osaka: 06-6941-9448
- Australian Embassy in Tokyo: 03-5232-4111
- British Consulate in Osaka: 06-6120-5600
- British Embassy in Tokyo: 03-5211-1100
- Canadian Consulate in Osaka: 06-6212-4910
- Canadian Embassy in Tokyo: 03-5412-6200
- Chinese Consulate in Osaka: 06-6445-9481
- Chinese Embassy in Tokyo: 03-3403-3065
- Indian Consulate in Osaka: 06-6261-7299
- Indian Embassy in Tokyo: 03-3262-2391
- Irish Consulate in Osaka: 06-6204-2024
- Irish Embassy in Tokyo: 03-3263-0695
- New Zealand Consulate in Osaka: 06-6373-4583
- New Zealand Embassy in Tokyo: 03-3467-2271
- South African Embassy in Tokyo: 03-3265-3366
- South Korean Consulate in Osaka: 06-6213-1401
- South Korean Embassy in Tokyo: 03-3452-7611

Information and Rating System

All information in this book was gathered through research, personal visits to each destination, exchange of information through local contacts, and reference to existing texts in Japanese and English (websites, brochures, books, onsite descriptions, etc.). I made a point of visiting each site before assigning it a rating, and also to consult with others and compare opinions in order to provide ratings that are as unbiased as possible. That said, as with any guidebook, information does change over time, so I cannot guarantee that small details will remain unchanged by the time you visit. I have endeavored to avoid errors and check all facts before publishing, but please keep in mind that I undertook this project by myself, at my own expense in terms of money and time.

As for the rating system, I use a simple and understandable scale ranging from 1 to 5, with 5 being a must-see for all visitors to Osaka, and 1 being something for expats living in Osaka who have seen most everything already, or who have a special interest in a particular aspect of Japan (traditional architecture, history, sports, etc.). The rating system was designed with the non-Japanese traveler in mind, and I tried to be as unbiased as possible, taking into consideration the wide range of interests people may have. The following can be used as a rough guideline:

- 5: The best of the best. This is something you cannot afford to miss, especially if you are visiting Osaka for the first time.

- 4: Excellent and well worth your time, especially if you have a particular interest in the type of site. If you have seen all the 5s, consider moving on to the 4s next.

- 3: There are many 3s that first-timers should consider visiting. A rating of 3 indicates a solid, quality destination that should be strongly considered.

- 2: A site rated 2 or below can probably be passed up by first-timers unless they have a specific interest in it or happen to be nearby. Local residents and repeat visitors, however, should highly consider taking a look at the 2s.

- 1: Even though this is the lowest rating, the fact that I included it in this guidebook means I consider it worth seeing. These are especially recommended for local residents as well as those who have seen most of the major sights of Osaka and want to delve deeper than the average tourist.

How the Sightseeing Guides are Organized

I have divided Osaka Prefecture into ten easy-to-understand zones to facilitate organization of the sights listed, and destinations within each zone are listed from highest-rated to lowest-rated (destinations with identical ratings are listed in alphabetical order). There are seven zones within Osaka City, and three zones in other parts of Osaka Prefecture, with most zones subdivided for easier understanding.

Osaka City Zones (7): Minami, Kita, Central Osaka City, Osaka Castle Area / Kyobashi, Tennoji / East Osaka City, West Osaka City / Bay Area, South Osaka City

Osaka Prefecture Zones (3): Southern Osaka Prefecture, Northern Osaka Prefecture, Eastern Osaka Prefecture

Along with place names in both Japanese and English, descriptions, costs, hours, directions, phone numbers, English-language websites (when available), phone numbers and other information is listed for each destination. Japanese addresses are also included for reference when applicable.

Making Use of the Internet and Phone Numbers: You can input phone numbers in online map software (such as Google Maps) or a GPS device to find their locations. This is particularly useful if you have Internet access on a mobile phone or other device while in Japan. You can also call the phone numbers listed if you get lost and want to ask for directions, but keep in mind that the English language skills of many people will be limited.

Interactive Online Content: The *Osaka Insider* blog features interactive maps showing all locations listed in this guidebook (http://osakainsider.wordpress.com/guidebook-maps). You can use these maps beforehand to plan your itinerary, print out sections of the maps to take with you, or access them on the go if you have a smartphone or compatible mobile device with Internet access.

Minami Sightseeing Guide

Overview

Minami (lit. "south") is the true center of Osaka, the dazzling, uber-urban mecca where you can find the best fashion and shopping, the best Osakan cuisine, the best nightlife, and a large number of the city's most famous sightseeing spots. Something new and amazing is around every corner, and the amount of shops, restaurants, bars and nightclubs is so great it would take a lifetime to see them all. Minami is the one part of town that never, ever sleeps, and its friendly denizens make sure that nobody feels like an outsider. In short, Minami represents everything that differentiates Osaka from the rest of Japan.

Namba

■ Dotombori and Ebisubashi (道頓堀・戎橋)

Rating: 5

Dotombori is one of Osaka's three most famous spots, and possibly the most well-known of them all. It is order in chaos, a maddening mix of people and lights and sounds that will assault your senses. *Lonely Planet* went as far as comparing it to the futuristic cityscape of Blade Runner.[4] But in my opinion, Dotombori has no comparison, because it is simply the city of Osaka unapologetically being its over-the-top self.

The name comes from the Dotombori River, a canal that runs east to west through the middle of the Dotombori district. Although

---

4 *Lonely Planet: Japan* 8th edition, p. 387

it was a theatre district starting in the seventeenth century, Dotombori is primarily a shopping and entertainment area today, so there are numerous bars, *izakaya*, restaurants, food stalls, and entertainments facilities (karaoke, video arcades, bowling, etc). The city has done extensive urban revitalization work in the area in recent years to boost tourism, focusing on beautification of the canal-side boardwalks. Namba's "love hotel" district can be found on the west end of Dotombori (near Yotsubashi-suji), offering a glimpse into another unique side of Japanese culture (and cheap lodging if you are traveling as a couple).

Famous landmarks include the giant crab with moving pincers (there are actually three, but the centermost one is the most popular); the night view of the Glico "running man" billboard; Ebisubashi Bridge (informally known as Hikkakebashi, meaning "pick-up bridge," as it is a popular spot for "hosts" who attempt to recruit girls passing by); the Ferris wheel on the side of the Don Kihote shop; and the view of the river itself from one of its many bridges. There is a Starbucks at the most crowded point in Dotombori, which offers a great view if you like people-watching or just want to take a breather. Boat tours go along Dotombori River and connect to other parts of Osaka (see next entry). Don't forget to pick up some affordable, delicious *okonomiyaki* (a popular type of savory Japanese pancake—see p. 159) and *takoyaki* (fried dumplings with octopus in the middle) from the outdoor food stalls near the river, as both of these are Osaka specialties.

➢ Access: The best way to reach the center of Dotombori is from Namba Station (Sennichimae and Midosuji Subway Lines, Kintetsu lines, Hanshin Namba Line, Nankai lines), but you can also get to the west part of Dotombori from Namba Station on the Yotsubashi Subway Line, and to the east part from Nippombashi Station (Sennichimae and Sakaisuji Subway Lines, Kintetsu lines). Dotombori is a 5 min. walk from Namba Station on the Midosuji and Sennichimae Subway Lines. Whichever station you exit from, walk north until you reach the Dotombori River.

■ Aqua Bus Tours (大阪水上バス)

Rating: 4

Operated by the Keihan Group, the Osaka Suijyo Bus ("Aqua Bus") sightseeing boat company operates various cruises around the city of Osaka, a place long known as "the City of Water" due to the historical significance of its canals and rivers. In fact, during the Edo Period (1600–1868), Osaka was the economic center of Japan, and powerful domain lords kept storehouses in Osaka for their rice in Osaka (rice was collected as tax and represented a domain's wealth)—the canals acted as the city's transport network for such goods, connecting warehouses and ports. Seeing Osaka from the water is a superb way to truly understand the character of the city. Cruises feature refreshments for sale and explanations of landmarks and scenery along the way, so they can be enjoyed by residents and tourists alike. Furthermore, cruises can be easily integrated into a city-center sightseeing itinerary, as the river routes connect some of the most popular spots in Osaka.

A variety of tours are available: The Aqua-Liner services operate frequently on a daily basis, providing river sightseeing cruises that stop at Osaka Castle (see p. 94), Tenmabashi (see p. 87), Yodoyabashi (see p. 86), and OAP (Osaka Amenity Park). Aqua Mini services cut north–south through the narrow Yokohorigawa River canal connecting the Okawa and Dotombori Rivers, stopping at Osaka Castle, Dazaemonbashi (in the center of the Dotombori entertainment district—see previous entry), and Minatomachi (a port near OCAT in Minami—see p. 57). The *Himawari* is a restaurant ship that departs from OAP and goes along the Okawa River. The *Santa Maria* is a replica of the ship of the same name, and it provides sightseeing cruises around Osaka Bay, departing from Osaka Aquarium Kaiyukan (see p. 115). The company also offers chartered cruises and special event cruises.

➤ Access: For Aqua-Liner cruises, which operate most frequently, the best port to start from is Yodoyabashi (near Yodoyabashi Station on the Midosuji Subway Line and Keihan Main Line), Hachikenyahama (near Temmabashi Station on the Tanimachi Subway Line and Keihan lines), or the Osaka Castle Park port (a short walk from Osakajokoen Station on the JR Osaka Loop

Line). The Minatomachi port (near OCAT (see p. 57) and Minatomachi River Place (see p. 60)) is close to JR Namba Station and Namba Station on the Yotsubashi Subway Line, and there is also a port in the middle of the Dotombori district (see p. 49). The *Santa Maria* departs from the back side of the aquarium (see p. 119).

➢ Cost: Aqua-Liner cruises range from 850 to 1,410 yen, Aqua Mini cruises cost 1,000 yen, *Himawari* cruises range from 4,725 to 8,925 yen (including a meal), and *Santa Maria* cruises are 1,600 yen during the day and 2,500 yen at night. Child tickets cost less than adult tickets. For details on pricing and departure schedules, please visit their website (see below).

➢ Phone: 05-7003-5551 (Aqua-Liner and Aqua Mini), 05-7044-5551 (*Santa Maria*), 05-7007-5551 (*Himawari*)

➢ Additional Information: http://suijo-bus.jp/language/english

■ Hozenji Yokocho (法善寺横丁)

Rating: 4

Hozenji Yokocho (Hozenji Alley) is hidden away in the backstreets of Namba, and its narrow lanes, old shops and stone-paved streets recall a past Osaka that has almost disappeared completely, swallowed by rapid urban development. Hozenji Yokocho was originally made famous by Osakan novelist Oda Sakunosuke's celebrated novel *Meoto Zenzai*, published in 1940. Hozenji Temple, after which the area is named, is a small but captivating temple dedicated to Amitabha. This temple is famous for its *mizukake fudo*, a moss-covered Buddhist statue that visitors throw water on when praying. It is said that women in the night trade go here before heading off to work, although you will mostly encounter visitors from the neighborhood and tourists. There are also a number of cozy cafes nearby. Drop by here for a truly local experience.

➢ Access: 5 min. walk from Namba Station (Midosuji, Sennichimae and Yotsubashi Subway Lines) or Nippombashi Station (Sennichimae and Sakaisuji Subway Lines). From Namba Station, take exit 15-A, turn around and walk the opposite direction along the boulevard once you ascend to ground level, and turn left at the second small street. You will soon see the entrance to your right. From Nippombashi Station, take exit 2, turn right and walk along the boulevard, and turn right at the fifth small street.

➢ Japanese Address: 大阪市中央区難波 1 丁目（付近）

■ Namba Parks (なんばパークス)

Rating: 4

This fantastic shopping center is connected directly to Nankai Namba Station and the Namba City building, and connected underground to subway and other rail lines. On the roof is a fantastic garden, a multi-tiered rooftop park cascading down the top of the terraced building with numerous walking paths hidden away amid lush greenery. There is a movie theater inside Namba Parks, some romantic restaurants, and a lovely night view of the illuminated cityscape, making it a popular date spot. Within the complex is a shop called Sho-Chu Authority, which specializes in *shochu*, *awamori* and other Japanese liquors and carries a wide variety of hard-to-find brands that will please any *sake* enthusiast. There is a wide selection of other shops and good restaurants, too, and Namba Parks is right next door to the massive Namba City shopping complex, which is also worth checking out.

➢ Access: The closest station is Nankai Namba Station on the Nankai lines, but Namba Parks can be easily accessed from any of the subway or other private railway lines (Kintetsu/Hanshin). JR Namba Station and Namba Station on the Yotsubashi Subway Line are a bit of a walk (about 10 min.). Both Namba Parks and Namba City are directly connected to Nankai Namba station.

➢ Open: Shops are open from 11:00 AM to 9:00 PM, and most restaurants from 11:00 AM to 11:00 PM.

➢ Phone: 06-6644-7100

➢ Japanese Address: 大阪市浪速区難波中 2-10-70

■ Namba Underground Shopping
(なんばウォーク・NAMBA なんなん地下商店街)

Rating: 4

Shinsaibashi to the north is known as the fashion mecca of Osaka, but Namba itself has plenty to offer. Osaka is a city where there is as much aboveground as there is hidden underneath, and the vast amount of shops and restaurants beneath the streets and sidewalks of Namba are proof of this—one can easily spend an entire day in Namba without ever seeing the sky!

Namba Walk is the largest underground shopping arcade, stretching all the way from JR Namba Station and Namba Station on the Yotsubashi Subway Line in the west to Nippombashi Station in the east. Other major shopping facilities, including the Takashimaya department store (see p. 56), Namba Parks (see previous entry), Namba City, OCAT (see p. 57), Bic Camera (a massive electronics store), Marui (see p. 57) and more can be accessed directly from Namba Walk. And don't forget to check out Namba Nan Nan, a smaller-scale arcade situated underground between the Midosuji and Sennichimae Subway Line stations and Nankai Namba Station. Whether it be food and drinks, the latest fashion, home decor, sporting goods, souvenirs, or anything else you can imagine, the underground shopping arcades of Namba have what you need.

➤ Access: You can get to these shops from any of the Namba Stations (subway, JR, Kintetsu, Hanshin, Nankai). The Midosuji and Sennichimae Subway Lines and Kintetsu/Hanshin lines are the most central for Namba Walk, and the Midosuji Subway Line and Nankai lines are closest to Namba Nan Nan.

➤ Open: Most shops and restaurants in Namba Walk are open from 10:00 AM to 9:00 PM (with some exceptions, including restaurants that are open until 10:00 PM); on certain months, the third Wednesday of the month is a business holiday. Namba Nan Nan store hours are essentially the same, and shops in Namba Nan Nan are closed for business holidays on the third Thursday of certain months.

➤ Phone: 06-6643-1641 (Namba Walk), 06-6631-5102 (Namba Nan Nan)

■ Osaka Prefectural Gymnasium (Sumo) (大阪府立体育館)

Rating: 4 (seasonal)

The original building was opened in 1952, and the current building was opened in 1987. This gymnasium is one of the four primary venues for sumo tournaments in Japan, and a major tournament is held in Osaka every March (the other three being in Fukuoka, Nagoya and Tokyo). Seeing live sumo is an unforgettable experience you can't afford to miss. Other sporting events, such as basketball games and pro wrestling matches, are also held here. The prefectural government surprised everyone in April 2008 with its plan to demolish the gymnasium (nothing has been officially decided upon yet), but that just means sumo will move somewhere else in the city. Until then, come to Osaka Prefectural Gymnasium in March to experience live sumo!

➤ Access: 3–5 min. walk from any of the Namba Stations (Midosuji, Sennichimae and Yotsubashi Subway Lines, Kintetsu lines, Hanshin Namba Line, Nankai lines) except JR Namba, from which it is a bit farther. From the west side of Takashimaya (see p. 56), continue along Midosuji Blvd., and after you cross under the elevated expressway, turn left at the third small street. You will soon see the gymnasium in front of you.

➤ Phone: 06-6631-0121

➤ Japanese Address: 大阪市浪速区難波中 3-4-36

■ Naniwa Yasaka Shrine (難波八阪神社)

Rating: 3

This shrine is located in the middle of Namba, a district whose name can also be read as Naniwa (see "Osaka History and Culture" on p. 30). Naniwa Yasaka Shrine is a typical small, local shrine in all ways except for one: the main shrine building is designed as a gaudy, 12-meter-high (39-foot-high) lion's head with piercing eyes and huge, golden fangs (see p. 19 for photograph). Most people are shocked the first time they turn the corner in this quiet neighborhood and see a giant face staring back at them through the small *torii* entrance gate. Naniwa Yasaka Shrine is worth a look because, well, there a few shrines in Japan as strange and amusing.

- ➤ Access: If you are taking the Midosuji Subway Line, get off at Daikokucho Station, take exit 2, turn left at the top of the staircase and walk north for 3–5 min., turn left at the "Motomachi 3 kita" intersection, turn right at the next signal, and look for the concrete *torii* gate on your left. If you are taking the Yotsubashi Subway Line, take exit 32 and walk straight (south) after exiting to ground level until you reach the "Motomachi 3 kita" intersection (about 5 min.), turn right at the next signal, and look for the concrete *torii* gate on your left.

- ➤ Phone: 06-6641-1149

- ➤ Japanese Address: 大阪市浪速区元町 2-9-10

■ Takashimaya Department Store (髙島屋)

Rating: 3

Takashimaya, founded in Kyoto in 1829, is one of Japan's most popular upscale department store chains, and the Osaka store (connected to Namba Station and various underground shopping complexes) boasts one the most elegant and iconic exterior designs of any of the stores in Japan. In total, Takashimaya has 18 domestic stores and 4 stores overseas (in New York, Taipei, Singapore and Paris).

Takashimaya has an abundance of upscale goods and the latest in fashion. You can find interesting souvenirs here such as *yukata* robes (staff will help you find the right size), toys, and of course food products and sweets on the basement level—even if you don't plan to buy food, there are plenty of free samples). Osaka's Takashimaya has seven storeys aboveground and one basement level.

- ➤ Access: Connected to Nankai Namba Station, and a 5 min. walk through underground corridors from Namba Station (Midosuji, Sennichimae and Yotsubashi Subway Lines, Hanshin Namba Line, Kintetsu lines).

- ➤ Open: 10:00 AM to 8:00 PM (dining from 11:00 AM to 11:00 PM)

> Phone: 06-6631-1101

> Japanese Address: 大阪市中央区難波 5-1-5

■ Marui (なんばマルイ)

Rating: 2

Marui is a Tokyo-based department store, and it's located right across the street from Nankai Namba Station and Takashimaya Department Store (see p. 56). Its famous logo consists of two circles and two lines rather than actual *kanji* characters, but because the circle can be pronounced "maru" and the line as "ee" in Japanese, local shoppers are able to read it. It is a popular store, especially among young people, because of its trendy fashion products.

> Access: Across the street from Nankai Namba Station, and directly outside exit 1 of Namba Station (Midosuji and Sennichimae Subway Lines).

> Open: 11:00 AM to 8:30 PM (open until 8:00 PM on weekends)

> Phone: 06-6634-0101

> Japanese Address: 大阪市中央区難波 3-8-9

■ OCAT (オーキャット)

Rating: 2

Osaka City Air Terminal (OCAT), while not an air terminal in actuality, is a transport hub for buses (highway buses and airport buses) and the JR Yamato Line (a rail line that connects Osaka and Nara). OCAT also has a number of stores and restaurants inside, and one store inside the complex, Yamaya, has a good selection of import foods and beverages. The appearance of OCAT is eye-catching, with one leg of the expressway entering into the building itself. Local dancers often gather in the plaza of OCAT (basement level) to practice their moves.

> Access: JR Namba Station is inside OCAT. If you are at any of the other Namba stations, it is a 5–10 min. walk through the

underground corridors. OCAT is located about 10 min. (on foot) west of most other sites in central Namba.

➢ Open: Shops are open from 11:00 AM to 9:00 PM, and restaurants are open from 11:00 AM to 10:00 PM (with some exceptions).

➢ Phone: 06-6635-3000

➢ Additional Information: http://www.ocat.co.jp/english.html

➢ Japanese Address: 大阪市浪速区湊町 1-4-1

■ Osaka Shinkabukiza (大阪新歌舞伎座)

Rating: 2

Osaka Shinkabukiza is the most well-known *kabuki* theatre in the region, and it features modern stage design innovations to support its top-class *kabuki* drama performances. The former theatre building was located in Namba on Midosuji Blvd., its decorative and eye-catching Momoyama-style architecture and massive scale making it quite a spectacle even from the outside. However, the building is no longer used for performances because the *kabuki* theatre was relocated in 2007 to the more modern YUFURA Uehonmachi Building (which also has office space and shopping facilities) to the east of Namba. When *kabuki* drama is not being performed, *manzai* two-person comedy, modern theatre drama, and variety shows are held at Shinkabukiza. I recommend taking a look at the old building while you are in Namba, and then taking the short train ride over to Uehonmachi to catch a show.

➢ Access: The old building is right outside exit 12 of Namba Station (Midosuji, Yotsubashi and Sennichimae Subway Lines, Kintetsu lines, Hanshin Namba Line), and it is a 2–3 min. walk from Nankai Namba Station. The current *kabuki* theatre is in the YUFURA Uehonmachi Building, which is directly connected to Osaka-Uehommachi Station on the Kintetsu lines, and also connected by underground corridor to Tanimachi 9-chome Station on the Sennichimae and Tanimachi Subway Lines (5 min. walk from the subway station). If you want to see the old building first, you can get between Namba and Osaka-

Uehommachi / Tanimachi 9-chome Stations in just a couple of minutes via the Sennichimae Subway Line or Kintetsu lines.

➢ Tickets/Schedule: Visit the website (in Japanese only—see below), call by telephone, or go to the theatre ticket window and ask directly (the latter is best if you don't speak Japanese).

➢ Phone: 06-7730-2121

➢ Additional Information: http://www.shinkabukiza.co.jp (Japanese only)

➢ Japanese Address: 大阪市天王寺区上本町 6-5-13 (current Shinkabukiza in Uehonmachi), 大阪市中央区難波 4-3-25 (old Shinkabukiza building in Namba)

■ Kamigata Ukiyoe Museum (上方浮世絵館)

Rating: 1

This small museum, located in a charming building in the old backstreets of Namba, displays a collection of *ukiyoe* woodblock prints, a unique form of artwork that has been popular for hundreds of years in Japan—even Vincent van Gogh was an avid admirer of Japanese *ukiyoe* prints. A large majority of Edo Period works (1600–1868) depicted *kabuki* drama actors, and in Osaka's booming Dotombori theatre district this type of artwork was particularly popular. Aside from works belonging to the museum, there are special exhibitions, and the third and fourth floors have displays of old photographs depicting the former Dotombori theatre district along with other items from that time.

➢ Access: 5 min. walk from Namba Station (Midosuji, Sennichimae and Yotsubashi Subway Lines) or Nippombashi Station (Sennichimae and Sakaisuji Subway Lines). Across the street from the entrance to Hozenji Yokocho (see p. 52).

➢ Cost: 500 yen for adults and 300 yen for middle school students and younger.

➢ Open: 11:00 AM to 6:00 PM (last admission at 5:30 PM). Closed on Mondays (or the next day if Monday is a public holiday).

- ➢ Phone: 06-6211-0303
- ➢ Additional Information: http://www.kamigata.jp/english
- ➢ Japanese Address: 大阪市中央区難波 1-6-4

■ Minatomachi River Place (湊町リバープレイス)

Rating: 1

This eye-catching, octagonal multi-purpose facility, located just outside the heart of Namba and near OCAT (see p. 57) and the ddd gallery (see p. 66), has gained popularity as a date spot. Besides serving as the main Aqua Bus sightseeing boat pier in Minami (see p. 51), it has a pleasant outdoor plaza that hosts musical performances and other events, the Namba Hatch concert hall inside, and the River Cafe restaurant. Although I only gave River Place a rating of 1 due to its lack of specific sightseeing attractions, it hosts some interesting events, and the illuminated nighttime scenery punctuated by the coming and going of boats makes it a superb spot to sit and relax, especially on hot summer nights.

- ➢ Access: 1–2 min. walk from Namba Station on the Yotsubashi Subway Line (exit 26-C) and JR Namba Station (across the street). It can also be reached easily from the other Namba stations via underground corridors connecting to exit 26-C.
- ➢ Open: The River Cafe is open from 11:30 AM to 4:30 PM, and 5:00 PM to midnight (last order at 11:00 PM). Times for other facilities vary.
- ➢ Phone: 06-4397-0571 (management office)
- ➢ Japanese Address: 大阪市浪速区湊町 1-3-1 (Namba Hatch)

Nipponbashi and Doguyasuji

■ Sennichimae Doguyasuji Shopping Arcade (千日前道具屋筋商店街)

Rating: 5

A walk through Doguyasuji is a unique experience anyone can enjoy. Restaurants in Japan often displays plastic models of menu items outside their shops to attract customers, and Doguyasuji is full of shops that sell these plastic food models. The manufacture of these items has reached what most would consider the level of art, as some of the higher-priced models are so realistic it's hard to discern between the plastic model and the real thing! Doguyasuji also sells illuminated shop signs, dishes and utensils, cooking equipment and tools, and everything else restaurant owners need to run their businesses. In cutlery shops, there are genuine, world-famous Sakai-made swords on display (and for sale, if you have a lot of money to burn). Overall, prices in Doguyasuji are quite reasonable, and some shops sell items in both large and small quantities, so you can buy something to take home as a souvenir. There are few places with so many unique and colorful stores all in one place, and because food culture is an essential part of Osaka (the city once known as the "kitchen of Japan") I highly recommend a stroll down Doguyasuji.

➢ Access: 3 min. walk from Nankai Namba Station on the Nankai lines; 3–5 min. walk from Namba Station on the Midosuji, Sennichimae and Yotsubashi Subway Lines, Kintetsu lines, and the Hanshin Namba Line; and 5–7 min. walk from Nippombashi Station on the Sakaisuji and Sennichimae Subway Lines and Kintetsu lines. From Namba Station on the subway or Kintetsu/Hanshin Osaka-Namba Station, exit onto Sennichimae-dori Blvd. (the east–west boulevard with an expressway running above), walk east until you reach Bic Camera, then turn right and walk straight through the Sennichimae Shopping Arcade until you reach Doguyasuji. From Nankai Namba, exit from the front of the station (ground level), turn right and walk until you see a shopping arcade entrance (near a Starbucks and underground shopping arcade entrance E5), then follow that shopping arcade and turn right at the first intersection inside, which should put you right in front of the entrance to Doguyasuji. From Nippombashi Station, walk west from the station down Sennichimae-dori Blvd. until you see Bic Camera, then turn left and follow the Sennichimae Shopping arcade until you see Doguyasuji.

➢ Open: Generally 9:00 AM to 6:00 PM (although individual shop hours may vary)

➢ Phone: 06-6211-0303

> Japanese Address: There is no single address. The best method is to follow the directions above or go to Namba Grand Kagetsu Theatre (see p. 64), which is located just outside the north end of Doguyasuji.

■ Den Den Town (でんでんタウン)

Rating: 4

Den Den Town is home for the Japanese *otaku*, a term that can be roughly translated as "geek" but actually has a broader meaning encompassing those obsessed with anything that can be obsessed about (robots, video games, manga, anime, movies, hardware, computers, etc.). The stores of Den Den Town are many and varied: there are specialty stores for anything you can imagine, even robots parts and flashing decorative lights, ranging in size from huge chain stores run by retailers such as Joshin and Sofmap to small shops with rare items you won't find anywhere else.

The main draw for tourists from abroad is the electronics stores, where the latest technology and gadgets can be seen before they go out from Japan to the rest of the world. Den Den Town is often compared to Tokyo's Akihabara, although many Japanese hold the opinion that Den Den Town has greater selection, better deals, and more personality. Besides electronics, the area is also a hub for lovers of manga and anime, and even for those who prefer stranger forms of entertainment such as "maid cafes."

Whatever your interests may be, Den Den Town has something to offer and should not be missed. There is a wide selection of duty-free shops for those who want to take something home.

> Access: Den Den Town extends along Sakaisuji Blvd. from north to south, and westward from Sakaisuji toward Nankai Namba station. Most of the video game, electronics, and media-related stores are concentrated in the south and middle portions, and the manga stores are closer to the Nankai Namba Station side. Ebisucho Station on the Sakaisuji Subway Line has exits right into Den Den Town (southern part), and Nippombashi Station (Sakaisuji and Sennichimae Subway Lines, Kintetsu

lines) puts you about 5 min. on foot to the north. You can also get there in 5–10 min. on foot from Nankai Namba Station and Imamiya-Ebisu Station on the Nankai lines, 3–5 min. on foot from Ebisucho Station on the Hankai Streetcar Line, and 10 min. on foot from Shin-Imamiya Station on the JR Osaka Loop Line and Dobutsuen-mae Station on the Midosuji and Sakaisuji Subway Lines.

■ National Bunraku Theatre (国立文楽劇場)

Rating: 4

The National Bunraku Theatre was opened in 1984 to preserve and develop *ningyo joruri bunraku*, or puppet theatre, as well as other arts of the Keihan region (Kyoto and Osaka). *Bunraku* is a traditional art form developed in Osaka in the late seventeenth century, and also one of Japan's most characteristic and fascinating forms drama; today it is designated as an Intangible Cultural Heritage by the Japanese government, and also recognized as such by UNESCO. In general, three puppeteers operate each puppet actor, executing precise movements of the hands, head, torso, and even mouth and eyebrows. Meanwhile, one or more chanters recite the lines while *shamisen* players provide musical accompaniment.

The National Bunraku Theatre's main hall is used mainly for *bunraku* performances and other stage drama, whereas the smaller one is used for *manzai*, *rakugo*, and the like. *Bunraku* plays generally run for two to three weeks, and there are five or so per year. These facilities are also used for other movements and projects aimed at preserving and promoting traditional Japanese arts.

A visit to Osaka provides an unparalleled opportunity to see *bunraku*, one of the world's most amazing art forms. The only reason I did not give this theatre a rating of 5 is that the shows do not have English interpretations; however, they are still thoroughly enjoyable for those who don't speak Japanese.

➢ Access: Just a few steps from exit 7 of Nippombashi Station (Sennichimae and Sakaisuji Subway Lines, Kintetsu lines).

> Tickets/Schedule: Contact the theatre or visit directly to find out about ticket costs and performance times. Information is available on the website (see below).

> Phone: 06-6212-2531

> Additional Information: http://www.ntj.jac.go.jp/english.html

> Japanese Address: 大阪市中央区日本橋 1-12-10

■ Kuromon Market (黒門市場)

Rating: 3

This fresh food market offers a wide selection of delicious seafood, vegetables, and other foods in its approximately 170 individual shops. The name "Kuromon" (lit. "black gate") refers to the black-colored gate of Enmeiji, a temple that was once located near this market. Local business owners visit Kuromon Market on a daily basis to stock up on ingredients, but there is plenty of good food to be enjoyed by individual shoppers as well. If you are in need for a tasty bite or some high-quality ingredients to cook with, or if you just want to experience a local neighborhood market in Osaka, Kuromon is the place to go.

> Access: 2–4 min. walk from exit 10 of Nippombashi Station (Sennichimae and Sakaisuji Subway Lines, Kintetsu lines). When you exit to ground level, continue down the boulevard in the direction you are facing until you see the market entrance on your left.

> Phone: 06-6631-0007

> Japanese Address: 大阪市中央区日本橋 2-4-1

■ Namba Grand Kagetsu Theatre (なんばグランド花月)

Rating: 2

Osaka is the capital of Japanese comedy, and Namba Grand Kagetsu (NGK) is Osaka's comedy mecca, a place where famous comedians and comedy groups perform every day. Besides *manzai* and *rakugo*, other types of performances such as musical performances and acrobatics can be seen here. Just steps away is the affiliated Base Yoshimoto, a comedy club for young performers—a gig here is arguably the best way to get your foot in the door in the Japanese comedy business. For a rare taste of live Japanese entertainment culture, and to experience performance arts in Minami (where Osaka performance arts were born), there is no better place to go than NGK. An understanding of Japanese, particularly Osaka dialect, is helpful when viewing performances here.

➢ Access: 3 min. walk from Namba Station on the Nankai lines; 3–5 min. walk from Namba Nankai Station on the Midosuji, Sennichimae and Yotsubashi Subway Lines, Kintetsu lines, and the Hanshin Namba Line; and 5–7 min. from Nippombashi Station on the Sakaisuji and Sennichimae Subway Lines and Kintetsu lines. From the subway or Kintetsu/Hanshin Osaka-Namba Station, exit onto Sennichimae-dori Blvd. (the east–west boulevard with an expressway running above), walk east until you reach Bic Camera, then turn right and walk straight through the Sennichimae Shopping Arcade until you see the theatre on your left. From Nankai Namba, exit from the front of the station (ground level), turn right and walk until you see a shopping arcade entrance (near a Starbucks and underground shopping arcade entrance E5), then follow that shopping arcade until the first intersection, from which you can see the theatre on your left. From Nippombashi Station, walk west from the station down Sennichimae-dori Blvd. until you see Bic Camera, then turn left and follow the Sennichimae Shopping arcade until you see the theatre on your left.

➢ Tickets/Schedule: Call or visit the theatre for ticket prices and performance schedules, or visit the website (Japanese only; see below).

➢ Phone: 06-6641-0888

➢ Additional Information: http://www.yoshimoto.co.jp/ngk (Japanese only)

➢ Japanese Address: 大阪市中央区難波千日前 11-6

Amemura and Kita-Horie/Minami-Horie

■ Amemura (アメ村)

Rating: 4

Amemura is a popular shopping and nightlife district located to the west of Shinsaibashi Station. It centers on Sankaku Koen (Triangle Park), a popular spot for skateboarders, dancers and other young people to gather day or night, and the area is also identifiable by a small replica of the Statue of Liberty (on top of one of the buildings). The district's name came from the various shops that started selling American import goods in the 1970s (Amemura is short for *Amerika-mura*, or "American Village"), and it features trendy imported and American-style fashion goods at prices that most likely only those interested in the absolute latest in style will consider paying. There is a scattering of galleries and shops selling accessories and various trinkets, and flea markets are sometimes held on weekends. For visitors, this spot is a great place to observe Osaka's youth culture, and it is also one of the best places to enjoy the city's nightlife (the most popular nightclubs are in and around Amemura). The area is also a popular gathering spot for local expats.

➤ Access: 5 min. walk from exit 7 or 8 of Shinsaibashi Station (Midosuji and Nagahori Tsurumi-ryokuchi Subway Lines), or 2 min. walk from exit 5 of Yotsubashi Station (Yotsubashi Subway Line). Amemura is situated between the two north–south boulevards Midosuji and Yotsubashisuji, and is almost equidistant (north and south) from Namba and Shinsaibashi/Yotsubashi Subway Stations.

➤ Japanese Address: Triangle Park's address is 大阪市中央区西心斎橋 2 丁目 11 番地. If you ask directions to "Sankaku Koen" (Triangle Park, written as 三角公園 in Japanese), most people will know what you are talking about.

■ ddd gallery (ddd ギャラリー)

Rating: 3

The ddd gallery, located in the Minami-Horie district, is a graphic art gallery managed by the DNP Foundation for Cultural Promotion. It has a sister gallery in Ginza (Tokyo) called the ginza graphic gallery (ggg). The ddd gallery holds various original art exhibitions by active artists throughout the year, and makes a humble but meaningful contribution to Osaka's art scene. Browsing the original works on display here is the perfect addition to a stroll through the posh restaurants and shops of Minami-Horie and Kita-Horie (see next entry).

➢ Access: 5 min. walk from Namba Station on the Yotsubashi Subway Line, and several minutes farther from Namba Station other subway and private rail lines. Take exit 26-C from Namba Station (near the Yotsubashi Subway Line and Kintetsu and Hanshin lines), walk across the bridge just to the north, turn left at the second traffic signal after crossing the river, and continue straight to the next intersection (the building is on the left).

➢ Cost: Free of charge

➢ Schedule: Call or visit the gallery for ticket prices and performance schedules, or visit the website (see below).

➢ Phone: 06-6110-4635

➢ Additional Information: http://www.dnp.co.jp/gallery/ddd_e/index.html

➢ Japanese Address: 大阪市西区南堀江 1-17-28 なんば SS ビル 1 階

■ **Kita-Horie and Minami-Horie (北堀江・南堀江)**

Rating: 3

After being mostly burned down during wartime bombings, this district was revived as a center for furniture sales. However, when business failed to pick up, it eventually declined, becoming gloomy and run-down. But from the 1990s onward, the area rebounded and began to gain popularity as a laid-back, mature alternative to the more youthful feel of nearby Amemura. Brand-name fashion shops came in from Tokyo, and the district developed into what it is now: a place brimming with chic cafes and dining bars and trendy clothing shops. Additionally, interior shops have emerged in great number, mainly on "Orange Street" (Tachibana-dori), the place where furniture-makers previously resided and did business. These districts are also unique for their upscale, one-of-a-kind bars and restaurants, which can be enjoyed day or night.

➢ Access: Kita-Horie is located near Nishiohashi Station (Nagahori Tsurumi-ryokuchi Line) and Yotsubashi Station (Yotsubashi and Nagahori Tsurumi-ryokuchi Subway Lines); the latter station is connected by moving walkway to Shinsaibashi Station on the Midosuji Subway Line. For Minami-Horie, walk 5–10 min. north from Namba Station (take exit 26-C near the Yotsubashi Subway Line and Kintetsu/Hanshin lines and follow Yotsubashisuji Blvd.), or walk north from JR Namba Station (across the street the from exit 26-C, which is connected underground to JR Namba Station).

Shinsaibashi

■ Shinsaibashi Shopping Arcade (心斎橋商店街)

Rating: 5

This is easily the most famous shopping arcade in Osaka, and possibly the most famous shopping district in Japan after Ginza in Tokyo. Located just one block east of Midosuji, it stretches for 600 meters all the way from Nagahori-dori (where Crysta Nagahori is located—see p. 70) to Dotombori in Namba (see p. 49). Shinsaibashi Shopping Arcade has a history of more than 380 years: the name Shinsaibashi comes from a former wooden bridge of the same name, and the area was historically a center of mercantile activity. There are approximately 180 shops of every sort in the shopping arcade, including clothing, fashion, lingerie, shoes, jewelry, coffee shops, restaurants, traditional Japanese sweets and tea shops, video arcades, pachinko parlors, and more. Furthermore, the entire arcade is covered by a roof, and it is even air-conditioned in the summer, so you can visit any time of the year.

Don't forget to stop by the Daimaru Department Store, where a wide selection of high-quality goods and gifts can be found, as well as Tokyu Hands, another department store that sells seasonal goods during the Christmas and Halloween seasons and other times of the year, as well as everyday lifestyle goods. Both of these stores are near the north end of the shopping arcade.

➤ Access: Directly outside of exits 5 and 6 of Shinsaibashi Subway Station (Midosuji and Nagahori Tsurumi-ryokuchi Subway Lines), or a few minutes' walk from Yotsubashi Station (Yotsubashi Subway Line, which is connected by moving walkway to Shinsaibashi Station). You can also get to the south end of this shopping arcade in about 5 min. on foot from Namba Station on the Midosuji and Sennichimae Subway Lines (located near Ebisubashi—see p. 49).

➤ Additional Information: http://www.shinsaibashi.or.jp/e /index.html (contains Shinsaibashi Shopping Arcade information, including a map of shops), http://www.tokyu-hands.co.jp/en/index.html (Tokyu Hands)

■ **Shinbashi Intersection (新橋交差点周辺)**

Rating: 4

The area surrounding Shinsaibashi Intersection on Midosuji Blvd. is home to a number of world-famous brand-name stores—Chanel, Dior, Armani, Gucci, Cartier, BLVGARI, Louis Vuitton, and Tokyu Hands, to name just a few. Daimaru Department store is also located here, occupying its original building as well a second building formerly belonging to the Sogo Department Store. Shinbashi Intersection is located right next to the Shinsaibashi Shopping Arcade (see previous entry), and directly above the underground Crysta Nagahori underground shopping complex (see next entry), serving as the luxurious centerpiece of the Shinsaibashi shopping district. In addition, there are plenty of restaurants, bars and clubs nearby for 24-hour entertainment.

➤ Access: Directly outside Shinsaibashi Subway Station (Midosuji and Nagahori Tsurumi-ryokuchi Subway Lines) at the intersection of Midosuji and Nagahori-dori Blvds. A few minutes' walk from Yotsubashi Station (Yotsubashi Subway Line, connected by moving walkway to Shinsaibashi Station).

> Japanese Address: 大阪市中央区南船場 3 丁目 （新橋交差点）

■ Crysta Nagahori (クリスタ長堀)

Rating: 2

This upscale and stylish underground shopping mall, built in 1997, is connected directly to Shinsaibashi, Yotsubashi and Nagahori Subway Stations, and also to the Shinsaibashi Shopping Arcade. It passes under Nagahori-dori Blvd., and water running underneath the street also goes through the roof and over the top of the ceiling windows of this shopping arcade—Nagahori was once a canal, but it was later filled in and turned into a boulevard, and this waterway serves as a reminder of the area's history. The mall stretches for 730 meters (almost half a mile) and contains approximately 100 fashion shops, restaurants and other commercial establishments mostly geared toward female tastes. You can also access the Daimaru Department Store directly from Crysta Nagahori.

> Access: Directly connected to Shinsaibashi Subway Station (Midosuji and Nagahori Tsurumi-ryokuchi Subway Lines) and Nagahoribashi Subway Station (Sakaisuji and Nagahori Tsurumi-ryokuchi Subway Lines). A few minutes' walk from Yotsubashi Station (Yotsubashi Subway Line, connected by moving walkway to Shinsaibashi Station).

> Open: 11:00 AM to 9:00 PM (closes at 8:30 PM on Sundays). Closed December 31, January 1 and the third Monday of February.

> Phone: 06-6282-2311

Kita Sightseeing Guide

Overview

Kita is the primary business district of Osaka, and it has shopping on par with that of Minami. Here you will find most of the city's largest department stores, as well as a labyrinth of underground shopping arcades and a behemoth shopping complex completed in 2011 that straddles Osaka Station. Although Kita lacks the uniquely "Osaka" character found in other parts of town, it does give you the full-scale Japanese urban experience, and it plays an important role as one of the Kansai region's largest transport hubs.

Sightseeing

■ Umeda / Osaka Station Area (梅田・大阪駅周辺)

Rating: 5

Umeda is one of the most popular places for shopping in Osaka, and people pour in from surrounding cities on weekends to catch the latest bargains or sip coffee at fancy cafes. The area has a wide gourmet selection and some of the most varied shopping available in Japan in all price ranges.

Four of Osaka's largest departments store are located here (Daimaru, Hankyu (my personal favorite), Hanshin and Mitsukoshi Isetan). Even if you are not interested in department store shopping, you should visit the basement levels to try free samples of various delicious foods from around Japan. The colossal JR Osaka Station City complex was completed in 2011, adding a handful of new shopping options to the area.

There is also a great number of underground shopping arcades beneath the streets of Umeda filled with restaurants, bars and stores—these include Whity, Diamor, Gare, Dojima, and the Hilton shopping complex. If you read Japanese, be sure to stop by the used bookstore area near Hankyu Umeda Station, or visit Kinokuniya (also near Hankyu Umeda Station) if you are searching for English-language reading material. For a panoramic night view while you eat, the Hankyu 32-ban Gai building and its wide selection of restaurants is the place to go. And make sure to take a look at Yodobashi Camera, one of the largest and most popular electronics stores in the city that also offers food and fashion shopping options.

Almost everything is connected by underground or overhead passageways in Umeda, and finding your way around can be confusing at first. Walking on street level lets you to see all the towering skyscrapers of Osaka's largest business district, and may make finding your destination much easier.

> Access: Umeda Station on the Hanshin Main Line, Hankyu lines and Midosuji Subway Line; Osaka Station on the JR lines; Higashi-Umeda Station on the Tanimachi Subway Line; and Nishi-Umeda Station on the Yotsubashi Subway Line. The Umeda Stations and JR Osaka Station are most central, while Higashi-Umeda Station puts you a bit more in the eastern area, and Nishi-Umeda Station puts you in the southwest near Kitashinchi (see p. 75).

■ Umeda Sky Building (梅田スカイビル)

Rating: 5

This building is an Osaka landmark and the main attraction of west Umeda. Its two towers, connected by a glass-enclosed escalator, are forty storeys high and feature indoor and outdoor observatories. The outdoor, open-air observatory on the top of the buildings, known as the "Floating Garden Observatory," is at an elevation of 170 meters (approximately 560 feet) and offers a stunning view of Osaka, the surrounding suburbs, and (on clear days) even Awaji Island. The observatory becomes packed on the morning of New Year's Day when people crowd on top to watch the first sunset of the year (a

Japanese tradition). Many events are held in and around the building, and the basement floor has a food court that re-creates the atmosphere of Osaka of the early twentieth century. The building itself, designed by architect Hiroshi Hara, is a marvel to look at from either far away or up close.

If you are in Umeda, a trip to the Umeda Sky Building is worth it for the view alone.

➢ Access: 10–15 min. walk from Osaka Station (JR lines) and Umeda Station on the Midosuji Subway Line, Hankyu lines and Hanshin Main Line.

➢ Cost: The Floating Garden Observatory costs 700 yen for adults, 500 yen for high school students, and 300 yen for students younger than that. Group discounts are available.

➢ Open: The Floating Garden Observatory is open from 10:00 AM to 10:30 PM (last entry at 10:00 PM). Hours may vary by season and during special events.

➢ Phone: 06-6440-3855 (observatory)

➢ Additional Information: http://www.kuchu-teien.com/english /index.html (Floating Garden Observatory)

➢ Japanese Address: 大阪市北区大淀中 1-1-88

■ **Chayamachi (茶屋町)**

Rating: 3

The Chayamachi district is geared toward young adults, as it is Umeda's center of cutting edge trends and fashions. NU chayamachi, a fashion-centered shopping complex, features the latest in clothing alongside an international selection of cuisine. Also check out Loft, a trendy store located behind NU chayamachi that sells various lifestyle products, home decor and seasonal goods. Next to Loft is a large video arcade where you might catch a glimpse of an outdoor Dance Dance Revolution competition during the warmer months. And during the winter holiday season, Christmas lights create a sparkling, romantic atmosphere on the streets at night near Loft. If you are in the mood for a drink, stop by the Chayamachi branch of the Hub, a popular English-style pub (there are five Hub pubs in Osaka).

> Access: 2–3 min. walk northeast from Umeda Station on the Hankyu lines (Chayamachi exit), 5 min. walk northeast from Umeda on the Midosuji Subway Line, and just a little farther walking north from Osaka Station on the JR lines and Umeda Station on the Hanshin Main Line. Approx. 10 min. walk from Higashi-Umeda Station on the Tanimachi Subway Line. Look for NU chayamachi as a landmark.

> Open: NU chayamachi and Loft are open from 10:30 AM to 9:00 PM. The Hub is open from 4:00 PM to 1:00 AM from Monday to Thursday, and open from 4:00 PM to 2:00 AM on Fridays, Saturdays and days preceding public holidays (happy hour is until 7:00 PM).

> Phone: 06-6373-7371 (NU chayamachi), 06-6359-0111 (Loft), 06-6376-8682 (Hub)

> Additional Information: http://www.eok.jp/restaurants-bars /group/chain/hub/ (Hub)

> Japanese Address: 大阪市北区茶屋町 10-12 (NU chayamachi), 大阪市北区茶屋町 16-7 (Loft), 大阪市北区茶屋町 3-4 チロル茶屋町ビル 2F (Hub)

■ Hankyu Higashidori (阪急東通商店街)

Rating: 3

Hankyu Higashidori is a network of shopping streets and shopping arcades that include various types of restaurants, bars, pachinko parlors, video arcades, karaoke establishments, *izakaya* and shops. The eastern section of this area has some rather seedy establishments (including an assortment of love hotels), but it also boasts some of the most original restaurants and bars in the Umeda area, so it's worth a look. Gyoza Stadium, where you can sample a wide variety of delicious *gyoza* dumplings, and popular ramen shop Hakata Ippudo (see p. 168), are nearby.

> Access: Near Umeda Station on the Hanshin Main Line, Hankyu lines and Midosuji Subway Line; Osaka Station on the JR lines;

and Higashi-Umeda Station on the Tanimachi Subway Line. One entrance is on the south side of HEP NAVIO (see next entry). Coming from the Osaka/Umeda Station side, Gyoza Stadium and Hakata Ippudo are behind HEP NAVIO (see next entry).

■ HEP FIVE and HEP NAVIO (ヘップファイブ・ヘップナビオ)

Rating: 3

HEP FIVE is the more popular of these two shopping centers, which are geared toward teenagers and young adults. HEP FIVE is decorated with two giant red whale sculptures, suspended from the ceiling and encircled by various floors of import and domestic fashion shops. Atop the building is the red, 106-meter-tall HEP FIVE Ferris wheel, an Umeda landmark that provides spectacular views of the city day or night. There is a large Toho Cinemas movie theater as well as additional shopping in HEP NAVIO, and both buildings have a moderate selection of restaurants and cafes to choose from.

➢ Access: 3–5 min. walk east from Umeda Station on the Hankyu lines and Midosuji Subway Line, and just a little farther from Osaka Station on the JR lines (walk east), Umeda Station on the Hanshin Main Line (walk northeast), and Higashi-Umeda Station on the Tanimachi Subway Line (walk north). The easiest way to get to HEP FIVE and HEP NAVIO is to find the 2F central exit ticket gates at Hankyu Umeda Station, go down the escalator/stairs in front of them to ground level (there should be a large TV screen labeled "BIGMAN"), turn left and walk out toward the street, then turn right and walk down the street until you see the two shopping complexes on your left (after passing under the elevated JR tracks).

➢ Cost: The HEP FIVE Ferris wheel costs 500 yen per ride (one ride takes 15 min.)

➢ Open: The Ferris wheel is open from 11:00 AM to 11:00 PM (last boarding at 10:45 PM). HEP FIVE opens at 11:00 AM, and stores close at 9:00 PM, amusement facilities close at 11:00 PM, and restaurants close at 10:30 PM. HEP NAVIO is open from 11:00 AM to 11:00 PM.

> Phone: 06-6313-0501 (HEP FIVE), 06-6316-1331 (HEP NAVIO)

> Japanese Address: 大阪市北区角田町 5 丁目 (HEP FIVE), 大阪市北区角田町 7 丁目 (HEP NAVIO)

■ Umeda Joypolis (梅田ジョイポリス)

Rating: 3

Sega's Joypolis, an amusement complex chain started in Yokohama, was opened in Umeda's HEP FIVE shopping complex in 1998. Primarily a video arcade, it also features amusement rides, simulators, *purikura* (photo booths where you can take photos with friends, modify and decorate them, and print them out in sticker form), and other entertainment for visitors of all ages.

> Access: Inside HEP FIVE (see previous entry).

> Cost: There are various combination tickets available, ranging from 1,600 to 2,200 yen per person.

> Open: 11:00 AM to 11:00 PM (last admission at 10:15 PM) every day

> Phone: 06-6366-3647

> Japanese Address: 大阪市北区角田町 5-15 HEP FIVE 8F・9F

■ Fukushima (福島)

Rating: 2

Located just southwest of Umeda (see p. 71) and west of Kitashinchi (see next entry), the Fukushima district has garnered praise in recent years one of the city's most fashionable gourmet hot spots. The district's tradition of delicious food from all over the world, however, precedes recent developments, as Fukushima has always been one of Osaka's best places for top-notch international cuisine. While restaurants in the area are not always as inexpensive as those in

Minami and other popular gourmet spots in the city, they provide food of the highest quality that will keep you coming back for more.

➢ Access: Fukushima Station on the JR Osaka Loop Line and Hanshin Main Line, and Shin-Fukushima Station on the JR Tozai Line.

➢ Note: The Fukushima district of Osaka should not be confused with Fukushima Prefecture in northeast Japan, which has become infamous overseas because of the 2011 nuclear power plant disaster. "Fukushima" is actually a very common place name in Japan.

■ Juso (十三)

Rating: 2

This district is located just outside central Osaka, on the opposite side of the Yodogawa River. It has a dirty past associated with yakuza, prostitution, and crime, but today it is much tamer and has some great restaurants serving genuine, tasty Osaka cuisine (be sure to stop in at Fukuya, one of the best *okonomiyaki* shops in town—see p. 163), as well as a friendly and welcoming neighborhood atmosphere. Think of it as a small-scale, down-to-earth version of Namba. While entertainment districts in Minami and Kita are better than Juso for first-time visitors, this is a good place to come if you have been in Osaka for a while and are looking for some variety. A popular fireworks festival is held at the Yodogawa River every summer (see p. 178).

➢ Access: Juso Station on the Hankyu Tazarazuka, Kobe and Kyoto Lines.

■ Kitashinchi (北新地)

Rating: 2

This district is located between Sonezaki (just east of Higashi-Umeda Station), Umeda (see p. 71) and Nakanoshima (see p. 81). It is Kita's liveliest nightlife district and contains a large number of lounges, bars, restaurants and clubs. The businesses operating here are almost all high-class establishments and cost quite a bit. While in Kitashinchi, be sure to stop by Inaba Harihichi (いなば播七), a Japanese sweets and *mochi* shop that has been in business since 1781. Tsuyuten Shrine (see p. 78) is also nearby.

➤ Access: Kitashinchi Station (JR Tozai Line) is closest, but it can also be reached from Umeda Station (Midosuji Subway Line and Hanshin Main Line), Nishi-Umeda Station (Yotsubashi Subway Line), Higashi-Umeda Station (Tanimachi Subway Line), and Osaka Station (JR lines).

➤ Phone (Inaba Harihichi): 06-6341-3266

➤ Japanese Address (Inaba Harihichi): 大阪市北区曾根崎新地 1-9-6 菱冨ビル 1F

■ **Ohatsu Tenjin (Tsuyuten Shrine) (お初天神／露天神社)**

Rating: 1

Ohatsu Tenjin has a history of about 1,200 years, and it became popular thanks to the *joruri* puppet-theatre drama *Sonezaki Shinju* (*The Love Suicides at Sonezaki*), written by celebrated Edo Period (1600–1868) playwright Chikamatsu Monzaemon. His drama was based on a double suicide that took place at Ohatsu Tenjin in 1703. The deities of this shrine are said to protect the Sonezaki and Umeda neighborhoods, and believers come here to pray for success in school and love. This popular shrine, hidden away in the backstreets of Osaka's largest business district, is worth a look if you happen to be in the area. A flea market, which is attended by many local residents, is held on the first Friday of every month.

➤ Access: 3–5 min. walk from Higashi-Umeda Station on the Tanimachi Subway Line or Kitashinchi Station on the JR Tozai Line. It can also be reached from other Umeda-area train and subway stations. From Higashi-Umeda Station, take exit 7 (exit H-82 according to the shopping complex's numbering), turn left from the exit and walk straight, turn left at the second small street you come to (near the large intersection), then go straight to enter the shrine grounds. From Kitashinchi Station, exit as far to the east as possible (on the Midosuji Blvd. side), cross the large "Umedashinmichi" (梅田新道) intersection, then turn left and walk straight until the second small street, turn right and enter the shrine (if you pass the Umeda OS Hotel on your right, you have gone too far).

➢ Phone: 06-6311-0895

➢ Japanese Address: 大阪市北区曾根崎 2-5-4

■ Shin-Osaka (新大阪)

Rating: 1

Although there are no tourist attractions here, the station has a number of shops for buying souvenirs and trying different foods, and it is a very convenient place to stay a night or two considering the lower price of hotels compared to more central parts of town and convenient transportation connections (the Shinkansen, or "bullet trains," stop here, as do subway and conventional JR line trains). There is an excellent selection of bars and restaurants in the area, so you won't run out of things to do at night. While I don't recommend this as a tourist attraction, it is a good place to do all your souvenir shopping if you haven't gotten around to it by the end of the trip (better than the airport stores).

➢ Access: Shin-Osaka Station on the JR Kyoto Line (also known as the Tokaido Line), JR Sanyo and Tokaido Shinkansen Lines, and Midosuji Subway Line.

■ Taiyuji Temple (太融寺)

Rating: 1

Founded in 821 by the revered monk Kukai, this Shingon-sect Buddhist temple is popular among residents of the Umeda and Ogimachi neighborhoods, and was also popular among shoguns and members of the imperial court in the past. New buildings were added to expand the temple, but they were burned to the ground in the 1615 siege of Osaka Castle by the Tokugawa and their allies (see p. 31), and after being rebuilt they were again destroyed during the 1945 allied firebombings near the end of World War II, so the current temple buildings are from the postwar period. An ancient thousand-armed Kannon statue and a stone Fudomyo-o statue are enshrined here, having survived both fires and warfare. The tomb of Lady Yodo, a concubine of Toyotomi Hideyoshi who killed herself during the 1615 siege, is also located in Taiyuji. Visitors to the temple pray to Fudomyo-o by focusing on a single request or wish while traveling in a circular path one hundred times around a pair stones on the temple grounds—similar to the method used at Ishikiri-Tsurugiya Shrine (see p. 155).

➤ Access: 5–7 min. walk from Higashi-Umeda Station on the Tanimachi Subway Line. It can also be reached from other Umeda-area train and subway stations. From Higashi-Umeda Station, take exit 6 (exit H-80 according to the shopping complex's numbering), turn right after leaving the exit at ground level, then take the first small street to your right (near the exit). Follow that street (going left when it branches in two), and after you cross a boulevard, continue along the same street until the fourth intersection (a T-intersection), where you will see the temple entrance on your left.

➤ Phone: 06-6311-5480

➤ Japanese Address: 大阪市北区太融寺町 3-7

Central Osaka City Sightseeing Guide

Overview

Ever since Osaka grew into a major trade center and castle town under Toyotomi Hideyoshi, the area stretching west from Osaka Castle has been the traditional city center and largely remains so today in terms of business, even if it is trumped by Kita and Minami in terms of entertainment and shopping. Aside from the area's wealth of museums and cultural venues, there are a number of retro-style historic buildings from the Meiji, Taisho and Showa Periods, as well as the lovely Nakanoshima riverine island, an urban garden of sorts in the midst of a field of skyscrapers. A visit here will also help you understand what Osaka was like in its early days, and also why it was called the "Venice of the East" in days past—board a sightseeing boat and see for yourself how different the city looks from the water! Tenjinbashisuji is also included in this section because it has stronger cultural and historical ties with this part of Osaka than with Kita (Umeda and vicinity are historically much newer parts of Osaka).

Nakanoshima

■ Nakanoshima Historical Buildings and Bridges (中之島の歴史散歩)

(Refer to walking map on p. 200)

Rating: 4

Nakanoshima is a long, narrow island located in the middle of two rivers, and it has been the traditional governmental administrative

81

center of Osaka throughout the city's modern history. The island is home to some beautiful, historical buildings with Meiji and Taisho Period architecture (1868–1926, when Japan first began to import European architectural styles), as well as numerous bridges with historical significance. Two of the most famous buildings are the Kokaido (officially known as the Osaka Central Public Hall; pictured on p. 14) and the Bank of Japan (pictured on p. 26) whose photogenic Osaka branch acts as the visual symbol of the Bank nationwide. You can also see Nakanoshima from the Aqua Bus sightseeing ferries (see p. 51), which offer views of the island's many bridges from atop the water and whisk you off to see other parts of the city.

The shores surrounding Nakanoshima were lined with warehouses and trading ports during the Edo Period (1600–1868), and the north shore's Dojima district was home to the first futures exchange in the world. The Museum of Oriental Ceramics (see p. 84), National Museum of Art (see next entry), and Osaka Science Museum (see p. 85) are located on the island, as is the city's biggest international convention center (Grand Cube Osaka). Thanks to efforts made by Osaka to increase tourist appeal, particularly in this area of town, and also thanks to the train line running underneath the island (opened in 2008, and built and operated by Keihan Electric Railway), Nakanoshima is on the path to becoming one of Osaka City's leading cultural hot spots. Be sure to take a look at the Kitahama and Yodoyabashi districts (see pp. 86, 200) and Nakanoshima Park (see p. 85) while you are in the area.

There is a detailed walking map on p. 200, which contains information on specific buildings, structures and facilities in the area.

➢ Access: Nakanoshima is accessible from Naniwabashi, Oebashi, Watanabebashi and Nakanoshima Stations (Keihan Nakanoshima Line); Higobashi Station (Yotsubashi Subway Line); Yodoyabashi Station (Midosuji Subway Line, Keihan Main Line); and Kitahama Station (Sakaisuji Subway Line, Keihan Main Line). Refer to the maps on pp. 200–201.

➢ Additional Information: http://osaka-chuokokaido.jp/english /index.html (Kokaido's website)

> Japanese Address (for Kokaido, a good place to start): 大阪市北区中之島 1-1-27

■ The National Museum of Art, Osaka (国立国際美術館)

Rating: 4

This museum was originally part of the Expo' 70 World's Fair in Suita City (in northern Osaka Prefecture—see p. 150), was reopened in 1977 as a regular museum, and was moved to its current site in central Osaka City in 2004 when its building in Suita was closed down and demolished. There are two exhibition floors filled with excellent works from inside and outside Japan (mostly postwar, with exceptions such as Picasso). Most of the building, a work of art in itself designed by Cesar Pelli, is completely underground, with the visible top section designed to resemble bamboo. The museum aims to encourage the development of contemporary art domestically and abroad.

> Access: 3–5 min. walk from exit 6 of Nakanoshima Station on the Keihan Nakanoshima Line (note: do not ride the Keihan Main Line; transfer to the Nakanoshima Line at Temmabashi or Kyobashi Station). 5–7 min. walk from Higobashi Station on the Yotsubashi Subway Line. 10 min. walk from Fukushima Station (Hanshin Main Line) and Shin-Fukushima Station (JR Tozai Line). From Nakanoshima Station (the closest station), take exit 6 and walk straight after exiting to ground level, turn right at the second traffic signal, and walk straight until you see the Osaka Science Museum on your right (the museum is adjacent to this building).

> Cost: 420 for adults, 130 for university students, and free for high school students or younger. Admission varies for special exhibitions. Group discounts are available.

> Open: 10:00 AM to 5:00 PM, but open until 7:00 PM on Fridays (last admission at 4:30 PM). Closed on Mondays (or the following day if Monday is a public holiday). Also closed between exhibitions and on certain other days. Please check the museum's website (see below) for details when planning your visit.

> Phone: 06-6447-4680

> Additional Information: http://www.nmao.go.jp/english/home.html

> Japanese Address: 大阪市北区中之島 4-2-55

■ The Museum of Oriental Ceramics, Osaka (大阪市立東洋陶磁美術館)

Rating: 3

This excellent museum, founded in 1982 and located near the Kokaido in the heart of Nakanoshima (see p. 81), features numerous works that are mainly Chinese and Korean in origin (with some Japanese works as well) and exhibits national treasures among its many pieces on display. The facility uses the latest in lighting and display technology to provide the best possible experience for visitors. About 1,000 years ago, this area of Osaka was the location of an important port where ceramics were imported from other parts of Asia, and the museum helps maintain this important cultural aspect of the surrounding district. The museum also has a "Tea Salon" with coffee, various teas, light meals and snacks. Written explanations in exhibitions are in English and Japanese.

> Access: Across the street from exit 1 of Naniwabashi Station on the Keihan Nakanoshima Line (note: do not ride the Keihan Main Line; transfer to the Nakanoshima Line at Temmabashi or Kyobashi Station). 5 min. walk from Kitahama Station (Sakaisuji Subway Line, Keihan Main Line), and just a little farther from Yodoyabashi Station (Midosuji Subway Line, Keihan Main Line). Refer to the maps on pp. 200–201.

> Cost: 500 yen for adults, 300 yen for college and high school students, and free for guests younger than that. Special exhibitions cost extra.

> Open: 9:30 AM to 5:00 PM (last admission at 4:30 PM). Closed Mondays (or the following day if Monday is a public holiday), during the New Year's holiday period, and between exhibitions.

> Phone: 06-6223-0055

➢ Additional Information: http://www.moco.or.jp/en
➢ Japanese Address: 大阪市北区中之島 1–1–26

■ Nakanoshima Park (中之島公園)

Rating: 1

As part of beautification efforts in central Osaka City, the metropolitan government has recently cleaned up and renovated this riverine-island park (first opened in 1891) and reopened it to the public. It has a rose garden that is popular in the summer, and in December it is decorated with gorgeous Christmas light displays as part of the Osaka Hikari-Renaissance holiday event (see p. 179). You can also sample food sold at outdoor stalls, day or night, during events and warm times of the year. Flanked by rivers on both sides, this park provides a refreshing green oasis amidst the towering buildings of Osaka's central business and administrative district.

➢ Access: Directly outside Naniwabashi Station on the Keihan Nakanoshima Line (note: do not ride the Keihan Main Line; transfer to the Nakanoshima Line at Temmabashi or Kyobashi Station), and a 3 min. walk from Kitahama Station (Sakaisuji Subway Line, Keihan Main Line).

➢ Additional Information: http://www.osaka-hikari.com/index _eng.html (Osaka Hikari-Renaissance website)

➢ Japanese Address: 大阪市北区中之島 1 丁目

■ Osaka Science Museum (大阪市立科学館)

Rating: 1

This museum is located above the underground National Museum of Art (see p. 83). It has four floors of mostly interactive science exhibits, an Omnimax theater, a planetarium, and live science demonstrations throughout the day. Kansai Electric Power donated a large amount money to fund the museum's construction (completed in 1989), and the museum focuses on the themes of "energy" and "the universe." It also has a large science library as well as scientific experiment facilities. This museum is primarily geared toward children.

> Access: Near Nakanoshima Station (Keihan Nakanoshima Line), next to the National Museum of Art (see p. 83).

> Cost: The museum costs 400 yen for adults, 300 yen for high school and middle school students, and is free for guests younger than that. The planetarium costs 600 yen for adults, 450 yen for high school and middle school students, and 300 yen for guests younger than that. Group discounts are available.

> Open: 9:30 AM to 5:00 PM (admission until 4:00 PM for the planetarium, and 4:15 PM for exhibits). Closed on Mondays (or next day if Monday is a public holiday), during the New Year's holiday period, and on facility holidays.

> Phone: 06-6444-5656

> Additional Information: http://www.sci-museum.jp/server_sci /en/info.html

> Japanese Address: 大阪市北区中之島 4-2-1

Traditional City Center

■ **Aqua Bus Tours (大阪水上バス)**

Rating: 4

(See p. 51)

■ **Kitahama/Yodoyabashi Historical Buildings (北浜・淀屋橋 歴史散歩)**

(Refer to walking maps on pp. 200–201)

Rating: 3

If you are interested in city walking, historic buildings and interesting architecture, this is probably the best place in Osaka to go. When I say historic buildings, I refer mainly to buildings from the late nineteenth and early twentieth centuries—the Meiji, Taisho, and

Showa Periods—when Japan was modernizing and starting to fuse its art and architecture with European aesthetics. There are older buildings from the Edo Period in the area, too.

Kitahama, Yodoyabashi and surrounding neighborhoods are home to numerous temples and shrines with historical significance, and other sites related to academic, mercantile and business culture in Osaka. Refer to the detailed walking maps on pp. 200–201, which contains information on specific buildings, structures and facilities in the area.

➤ Access: Kitahama Station (Sakaisuji Subway Line, Keihan Main Line), Yodoyabashi Station (Midosuji Subway Line, Keihan Main Line), Hommachi Station (Midosuji, Chuo and Yotsubashi Subway Lines), and Sakaisuji-Hommachi Station (Sakaisuji and Chuo Subway Lines). Refer to the walking maps on pp. 200–201.

■ Tenmabashi and Hachikenyahama (天満橋・八軒家浜)

Rating: 2

This riverfront business district has a wide variety of restaurants and shops (in and around Temmabashi Station), most of them in the two major shopping and office complexes of Keihan City Mall and the Osaka Merchandise Mart (OMM). There are also many exquisite French and Italian restaurants in a quiet residential neighborhood not far from the station (cross Tosabori-dori Blvd., the smaller of the two boulevards, walk west toward Kitahama, turn left at the staircase and climb up to find them), as well as along Tosabori-dori Blvd. itself (walk west from the station toward Kitahama). The Okawa Riverfront has recently undergone redevelopment as part of the city's efforts to revive Osaka as the "city of water," and Hachikenyahama Pier (located behind Temmabashi Station) has been newly renovated to handle more sightseeing boats and events. In spring, the banks of the Okawa River come to life with pink and white cherry blossoms, and at night throughout the year the riverbanks are beautifully illuminated. If you don't mind splurging, try the upscale Kawa no Eki Hachikenya restaurant, which offers river-view seats and top-notch French cuisine.

Tenjin Matsuri (see p. 177), one of Japan's biggest festivals, takes place near Temmabashi Station, as do other events throughout the year. The area is also within walking distance of Osaka Castle Park (see p. 94).

➤ Access: Temmabashi Station (Tanimachi Subway Line, Keihan lines).

➤ Phone: 06-6944-5088 (Keihan City Mall), 06-6943-2020 (OMM)

➤ Additional Information: http://www.osaka-info.jp/tenjin _matsuri/main_en.html (Tenjin Matsuri website)

➤ Japanese Address: 大阪市中央区天満橋京町 1-1 (Keihan City Mall), 大阪市中央区大手前 1-7-31 (Osaka Merchandise Mart), 大阪市中央区北浜東 1-6 (Kawa no Eki Hachikenya)

■ Utsubo Park (靱公園)

Rating: 2

This area was a fresh fish wholesale market from the Edo Period (1600–1868) until the 1930s, and after World War II it was used for a short time as a US Army airfield, which explains its long, rectangular runway shape. Today, it is a pleasant park frequented by local businesspeople and residents alike. Its fragrant rose garden is the oldest such garden in Osaka and features an astonishing variety of colorful flowers along with a beautiful fountain. At night, you can walk along the romantic, lamp-lit paths from one end to another and enjoy the night air. There are 16 tennis courts on the west end, which are used for tournaments but are also available for regular use.

➤ Access: 5 min. walk north from Hommachi Station on the Yotsubashi, Chuo and Midosuji Subway Lines (take exit 28, which is closest to the Yotsubashi Line, and walk straight after exiting to ground level). The tennis courts on the west end are a 5 min. walk north from Awaza Station on the Chuo Subway Line (take exit 1).

➤ Phone: 06-6441-6748

➤ Japanese Address: 大阪市西区靱本町 1-9

■ Yamamoto Noh Theatre (山本能楽堂)

Rating: 2

This theatre was originally built in 1921 by the late Hiroyuki Yamamoto, and rebuilt in 1950 after it was burned down during World War II. Thanks to the preservation of the Noh drama tradition and its long service to the cultural arts, the theatre was designated by the government as a tangible cultural heritage in 2006. This facility aims to preserve and spread the tradition of Noh theatre (also known as Nogaku or Nohgaku), an important form of drama originating in Japan and designated as an intangible cultural heritage by UNESCO.[5] The theatre has a traditional wooden stage with empty pots placed underneath to create sound effects during performances (an old technique), as well as a lovely tea room. Aside from Noh performances, visitors can participate in acting classes with Noh performers and watch other forms of traditional performance hosted by the theatre. A one-hour stage tour is also available for 1,000 yen per person. Yamamoto Noh Theatre is appropriately located near Osaka Castle, the base of power of famous former shogun Toyotomi Hideyoshi, who was an avid fan and supporter of Noh drama. Come see for yourself why Noh theatre has been an important part of Japanese culture for more than 700 years.

➤ Access: 3 min. walk from exit 4 of Tanimachi 4-chome Station (Chuo and Tanimachi Subway Lines). From exit 4, walk straight down the small street in front of you, take the first right, then take a left, after which the theatre will be visible on your left side.

➤ Tickets/Schedule: Check the website, contact the theatre, or visit directly to find out about ticket costs and performance times.

➤ Phone: 06-6846-3369

➤ Additional Information: http://www.noh-theater.com/english /eng_welcome.html

➤ Japanese Address: 大阪市中央区徳井町 1-3-6

---

[5] http://www.unesco.org/culture/ich/index.php?lg=en&pg=00011&RL=00012

■ Semba Center Building (船場センタービル)

Rating: 1

This massive structure, a one-kilometer section underneath the elevated Hanshin Expressway, is divided into ten buildings with approximately 1,000 shops and restaurants. Wholesale goods, fashion products, accessories, shoes, import goods and many other products are sold in this vast shopping complex. There is also a number of independent wholesalers who sell to local vendors. While the buildings themselves are not particularly stylish or flashy, they are full of unique shops offering unbeatable deals, and the convenient central location makes it easy to stop by any time. The basement levels also host a wide selection of restaurants. If you want to get a taste of real, modern-day Osaka merchant culture, pay a visit to the Semba Center Building.

➢ Access: Directly connected to Hommachi Station (Midosuji, Yotsubashi and Chuo Subway Lines) and Sakaisuji-Hommachi Station (Sakaisuji and Chuo Subway Lines).

➢ Open: Varies by shop, but most shops are small businesses run by one or two staff members, so don't expect late business hours (with the exception of some restaurants).

➢ Phone: 06-6281-4500

➢ Japanese Address: 大阪市中央区船場中央 1 丁目〜4 丁目

Tenjinbashisuji

■ Osaka Museum of Housing and Living
(住まいのミュージアム 大阪くらしの今昔館)

Rating: 4

In this one-of-a-kind facility, you have an opportunity to experience life in the Edo Period (1600–1868) by walking through a re-created section of old Osaka, complete with shops, houses, period furniture and appliances, and even lighting changes to simulate different times of the day and night. Performers put on shows using *shamisen* and other traditional instruments in a *tatami*-mat room in one of the town's buildings. After you've wandered through re-created shops, houses and back alleys, continue on to the museum section to learn about Osaka in the modern and contemporary periods through video footage, exhibited objects, scale models and more. As its name implies, this museum gives visitors a fascinating peak into the way people lived (and the places they lived in) by immersing them in the past itself. For a day of tourism with a culture and history theme, try combining a visiting to the Osaka Museum of Housing and Living with a trip to the Osaka Museum of History (see p. 96)!

➤ Access: Directly outside exit 3 of Tenjimbashisuji 6-chome Station (Tanimachi and Sakaisuji Subway Lines, Hankyu Senri Line). 10 min. walk north from Temma Station on the JR Osaka Loop Line (follow the Tenjinbashisuji Shopping Arcade).

➤ Cost: 600 yen for adults, 300 yen for university and high school students, and free for middle school students and younger. Special exhibitions cost extra, and group discounts are available.

➤ Open: 10:00 AM to 5:00 PM (last admission at 4:30 PM). Closed on Tuesdays (next day instead if Tuesday is a public holiday), days following public holidays (except for Sundays and Mondays), every third Monday of the month, during the New Year's holiday period, and on occasional facility holidays.

➤ Phone: 06-6242-1170

➤ Additional Information: http://www.city.osaka.lg.jp/contents /wdu020/toshiseibi/english/museum.html

➤ Japanese Address: 大阪市北区天神橋 6-4-20

■ **Tenjinbashisuji Shopping Arcade (天神橋筋商店街)**

Rating: 3

This shopping arcade lies along a pilgrimage route to Tenmangu Shrine—a route with a history going back approximately 1,000 years. The shopping arcade extends for a distance of 2.6 kilometers (1.6 miles), making it Japan's longest, and it hosts a wide variety of restaurants, *izakaya*, shops and food stalls. Unlike other shopping arcades in the city, this arcade acts as a sort of "town center" to residents in nearby neighborhoods, and as a result it has a more down-to-earth, local feel. Tenma Tenjin Hanjotei, a famous *rakugo* (Japanese comedy) theatre, is located here, and Tenmangu Shrine (see next entry) is right next door. To see how people lead their lives every day in Osaka, as well as grab a delicious bite to eat, you can't go wrong with the Tenjinbashisuji Shopping Arcade. And like most shopping arcades in Osaka, it is covered by a roof so you can visit even on rainy days.

➢ Access: Minami-morimachi Station (Tanimachi Subway Line) and Osakatemmangu Station (JR Tozai Line) are connected to each other, and either of these will put you at the southern end of the shopping arcade (exit 3). To start from the northern end, get off at Tenjimbashisuji 6-chome Station (Tanimachi and Sakaisuji Subway Lines, Hankyu Senri Line) and take exit 9, and to start in the middle, get off at Ogimachi Station (Sakaisuji Subway Line; take exit 1) or Temma Station (JR Osaka Loop Line).

■ Osaka Tenmangu Shrine (大阪天満宮)

Rating: 2

Originally constructed in 949, Osaka Tenmangu Shrine is one the most famous Tenjin Shrines in Japan, and it hosts the Tenjin Matsuri every July, a great festival that is considered to be one of the top three in the country (see p. 177). The shrine's deities are said to grant believers success and growth in scholarship, and the shrine serves the local neighborhood by hosting numerous events and festivals. Inside, there is a small walk-through exhibit (free of charge) on the shrine's history, and the ornamental interior of the main hall and the stately gate at the south entrance to the complex are worth seeing. It is best to visit this shrine during the Tenjin Matsuri (if you don't mind crowds), but it can also be combined with a trip to the Tenjinbashisuji Shopping Arcade (see previous entry).

➢ Access: 3–5 min. from exit 4-B of Minami-morimachi Station (Tanimachi Subway Line) and Osakatemmangu Station (JR Tozai Line). Take the elevator near exit 4-B up to ground level, enter the shopping arcade to your left, take the second street on you see on the left (small street), and from there continue going straight until you see the shrine on your left.

➢ Open: 9:00 AM to 5:00 PM

➢ Phone: 06-6353-0025

➢ Japanese Address: 大阪市北区天神橋 2-1-8

Osaka Castle Area / Kyobashi Sightseeing Guide

Overview

Osaka Castle was once the greatest fortress in Japan, and today it is still one of Osaka City's most important symbols. The castle and the area surrounding it have an abundance of historical and cultural value, making them a must-see during any visit to Osaka City. Nearby is Osaka Business Park, a chic business complex with restaurants boasting views of the castle. And Kyobashi, one of the city's biggest subcenters and home to down-to-earth *shitamachi* culture and cuisine, is only a short distance away.

Sightseeing

■ Osaka Castle Park (大阪城公園)

Rating: 5

Osaka Castle was built by Toyotomi Hideyoshi, a great leader in the late sixteenth century who rose from peasantry to become one of the three unifiers of Japan and help end a long, bloody period of feudal warfare. It was the greatest, most intimidating castle in Japan at the time, and it provided the catalyst for the growth of Osaka, the merchant's capital and economic engine of Japan during the Edo Period (1600–1868). Hideyoshi's son, Hideyori, would resist the shogun who took power after his father's death, and defend against two assaults using Osaka Castle as a base before committing suicide with his mother when the battle was lost. Hideyoshi's castle was destroyed after the battle, and once again during a fire; the current structure is a faithful reconstruction from the 1930s (renovated in 1997 to re-create the feel of original castle even more closely). The moats and walls are almost completely original—the huge boulders making up the walls are held together by sheer weight alone!—as is one of the turrets. The interior of the castle has been turned into an informative and interesting history museum, where you can learn about the assaults on the castle and see feudal armor and weaponry up close. Additionally, the view from the top of the keep provides a sweeping view of the city. The surrounding park is gorgeous, especially when the cherry blossoms or plum blossoms are in full bloom, and when the autumn colors set the green landscape ablaze with reds and yellows. Hokoku Shrine, one of the many temples built to honor Hideyoshi, is located inside the park.

Some people criticize Osaka Castle because it is a modern reconstruction. Without getting into a deep discussion about the true significance of historical monuments, I would argue that Osaka Castle still plays several of the roles it was intended to play—namely, that of impressing onlookers, and of acting as a symbol of Toyotomi power and of Osaka. Aside from the castle itself, the spacious park (one of Japan's most well-planned parks), event facilities (Osaka-jo Hall and others) and sightseeing boat pier (see p. 51) make Osaka Castle Park a must-see sightseeing destination.

➢ Access: Directly outside Morinomiya Station (Chuo and Nagahori Tsurumi-ryokuchi Subway Lines, JR Osaka Loop Line), 5 min. walk from Tanimachi 4-chome Station (Tanimachi and Chuo Subway Lines), 5 min. walk from Temmabashi Station (Tanimachi Subway Line, Keihan lines), 10 min. walk from Osakajokitazume Station (JR Tozai Line), 10–15 min. walk from Kyobashi Station (JR Osaka Loop Line, JR Tozai Line, JR Gakkentoshi Line / Katamachi Line, Keihan lines, Nagahori Tsurumi-ryokuchi Subway Line), 5 min. walk from Osaka Business Park Station (Nagahori Tsurumi-ryokuchi Subway Line), and 5 min. walk from Osakajokoen Station (JR Osaka Loop Line). In additional, Aqua Bus sightseeing boats (see p. 51) stop at the park's river port.

➢ Cost: the Osaka Castle Museum costs 600 yen for adults, and is free for guests 15 years of age or younger. There are also group discounts. The park itself is free.

- Open: Osaka Castle, which has a museum and an open-air observatory on top, is open from 9:00 AM to 5:00 PM (last admission at 4:30 PM), and open later during busy tourist seasons (Golden Week, summer break, etc.). It is closed from December 28 to January 1. The park itself is open at all times.

- Phone: 06-6941-3044

- Additional Information: http://www.osakacastle.net/english

- Japanese Address: 大阪市中央区大阪城 1-1

■ Osaka Museum of History (大阪歴史博物館)

Rating: 5

This superb museum, an NHK project, covers Osaka's rich 1,400-year history from the its early days as the imperial capital Naniwa-kyo, through the Edo Period when it was the economic and mercantile center of the country, to its modern period when it became a center stage for revolutionary social change and an industrial engine for the nation, and finally to its contemporary period. Priceless artifacts are mixed with interactive media displays and faithful re-creations and models (including a full-sized replica of the interior of the ancient Naniwa Palace) that not only teach but entertain by showing how truly fascinating Osaka's history can be, making for a museum that appeals to a wider audience than just history fanatics. From the museum, you can also take in an unparalleled bird's-eye view of the grounds of Osaka Castle (see previous entry) and the neighboring Naniwa Palace ruins (see p. 100). If you only go to one museum in Osaka, this should be the one.

- Access: 5 min. walk from Tanimachi 4-chome Station on the Chuo Subway Line (exit 9).

- Cost: 600 yen for adults, 400 yen for university and high school students, and free for guests younger than that. Special exhibitions may cost extra. Group discounts are available.

- Open: 9:30 AM to 5:00 PM (until 8:00 PM on Fridays; last admission at 4:30 PM). Closed on Tuesdays (or the next day if Tuesday is a public holiday) and from December 28 to January 4.

> Phone: 06-6946-5728

> Additional Information: http://www.mus-his.city.osaka.jp
> /english_iso-8859-1/index.html

> Japanese Address: 大阪市中央区大手前 4-1-32

■ **Aqua Bus Tours (大阪水上バス)**

Rating: 4

(See p. 51)

■ **Peace Osaka (Osaka International Peace Center) (ピース
おおさか 大阪国際平和センター)**

Rating: 4

In 1945, aside from the two atomic bombings of Hiroshima and
Nagasaki, 66 major Japanese cities were targeted by B-29 bomber
squadrons carrying incendiary bombs designed to burn down
Japanese buildings, which were mostly made using wood and paper
at the time. These 66 cities, including Osaka, were almost
completely demolished. Hundreds and thousands were killed in the
bombings, and the economy and infrastructure of the country were
reduced to shambles.[6]

Osaka International Peace Center, more commonly known as
Peace Osaka, features a number of exhibits on subjects including the
firebombings of Osaka, the expansion of the Japanese Empire in
Asia during World War II and the harm it brought to many countries,
and other important topics. There are heartbreaking video clips taken
from the B-29s showing bombs being dropped, images of the city in
ruins afterwards, items salvaged from the rubble, and many
revealing testimonies and explanations of historical events of the
time. As Peace Osaka's name implies, this museum aims to provide
an unbiased view of the wartime destruction with the goal of
reminding people of the mistakes of the past to prevent history from

---

[6] *Overall Report of Damage Sustained by the Nation During the Pacific War.* Economic Stabilization
Agency, Planning Department, Office of the Secretary General, 1949.

repeating itself. Just like the Hiroshima Peace Memorial Museum and other such facilities throughout Japan, Peace Osaka delivers and an important anti-war message. Be warned that some of the images are quite graphic and disturbing, as is generally the case with any honest portrayal of the realities of war.

> Access: 3–5 min. walk from exit 1, or 2–3 min. walk from exit 3-B, of Morinomiya Station on the Chuo and Nagahori-tsurumi Subway Lines, and 3–5 min. walk from Morinomiya Station on the JR Osaka Loop Line.

> Cost: 250 yen for adults, 150 yen for high school students, and free for middle school students or younger, senior citizens (age 65 or older) and handicapped guests. A group discount is available.

> Open: 9:30 am to 5:00 pm (closed Mondays, days following public holidays, the last day of each month, and during the New Year's holiday period). Entry is allowed until 30 min. before closing time.

> Phone: 06-6947-7208

> Additional Information: http://www.peace-osaka.or.jp/pdf /pamphlet_en.pdf

Japanese Address: 大阪市中央区大阪城 2-1

■ Fujita-tei Remains Park and Museum (藤田邸跡公園・藤田美術館)

Rating: 2

Fujita Denzaburo was born in Yamaguchi Prefecture, and after participating in the Meiji Restoration (a relatively non-violent revolution that resulted in the creation of a parliamentary government), he moved to Osaka in the early Meiji Period (1868–1912) and achieved great success as a businessman in mining, spinning, military supply and other fields, helping build the foundations of Osaka's modern economy. The main attraction of this site is the garden built by Fujita, which has been restored to remind us that Fujita was also active in cultural activities. It centers on a charming pond, filled with brightly colored carp and sheltered in the shade of tree branches. There is also a small museum of East Asian art on the grounds.

The nearest station is Osakajokitazume, but for travelers with extra time on their hands, I recommend getting off at Temmabashi Station, walking along Tosabori-dori Blvd. until you reach the pedestrian bridge that crosses over into Osaka Castle Park (near the brick Nikkei newspaper building), then turning left at that point and crossing under the Keihan railroad tracks and following the river path (turn right after the tracks) until you reach the Fujita-tei Remains. It is a 20–30 min. walk, but it is a pleasant one featuring some refreshing Okawa River scenery.

➤ Access: Right outside exit 3 of Osakajokitazume Station (JR Tozai Line), or a 20–30 min. walk northeast from Temmabashi Station (Tanimachi Subway Line, Keihan lines) or southwest from Kyobashi Station (JR Osaka Loop Line, JR Tozai Line, JR Gakkentoshi Line / Katamachi Line, Nagahori Tsurumi-ryokuchi Subway Line, Keihan lines).

➤ Cost: Admission to the museum is 800 yen per person. Viewing the garden is free.

➤ Open: The art museum is open from 10:00 AM to 4:30 PM (closed on Mondays).

➤ Phone: 06-6351-0582 (museum)

➤ Japanese Address: 大阪市都島区網島町 10-32

■ **Kyobashi (京橋)**

Rating: 1

This is one of Osaka's major urban subcenters, located near Tenmabashi, Osaka Business Park and Osaka Castle (see previous entries in this section). While it is most well-known for its numerous love hotels and shot bars (and some good bars if you are looking for a quieter scene than Minami), it is also home to a number of businesses and original restaurants and bars. Parts of nighttime Kyobashi are a bit sleazy, but the area is relatively safe and can be a lot of fun at night. There is plenty of great shopping at the Keihan

Mall and Keihan Department Store, and there is also a good selection of cafes and restaurant where you can take a quick breather.

➤ Open: Keihan Mall's shopping facilities are open from 10:30 AM to 9:00 PM, its restaurants are open from 11:00 AM to 11:00 PM (some restaurant hours may vary), and its basement-level food floor is open from 10:00 AM to 8:00 PM. The Keihan Department Store is open from 10:00 AM to 9:00 AM (restaurants are open from 10:30 AM to 9:00 PM).

➤ Phone: 06-6353-2525 (Keihan Mall), 06-6355-1313 (Keihan Department Store)

➤ Access: Kyobashi Station on the JR Osaka Loop Line, JR Tozai Line, JR Gakkentoshi Line / Katamachi Line, Nagahori Tsurumi-ryokuchi Subway Line, and Keihan lines.

■ Naniwa Palace Historical Park (難波宮跡公園)

Rating: 1

Naniwa-kyo (the former name of Osaka) was the imperial capital in ancient times, and Naniwa Palace was first built in 645, was burned down, and was later rebuilt in a nearby location in 726. Not only was Naniwa Palace used as the headquarters of Japanese emperors, it functioned as a hall for foreign dignitaries (primarily from China) even after the Japanese imperial capital was moved to Heijo-kyo (Nara) and then Heian-kyo (Kyoto).

The foundation of the second palace's Daigokuden Hall has been restored in this mid-sized park adjacent to Osaka Castle Park (see p. 94) and the Osaka Museum of History (see p. 96). While the park in itself is not overly impressive, its historical significance can be appreciated following a visit to the fascinating Osaka Museum of History. Many of the artifacts from the museum were excavated from this location, which is where the palace was actually located. This historical site serves as a reminder of Osaka's fascinating and complex past, and its importance in shaping Japanese history as a whole.

➤ Access: 2 min. walk from exit 10 of Tanimachi 4-chome Station (Chuo and Tanimachi Subway Lines). It is located very close to

Osaka Castle Park (see p. 94) and the Osaka Museum of History (see p. 96).

➤ Japanese Address: 大阪市中央区法円坂 1 丁目

■ Osaka Business Park (大阪ビジネスパーク)

Rating: 1

Osaka Business Park (OBP for short) is a modern, photogenic cluster of skyscrapers that offers a modern backdrop for Osaka Castle. The business park's centerpiece, the mirror-like Crystal Tower, changes appearance with the weather and time of day, often taking on a rich blue tint as it reflects the sky above. The headquarters of Yomiuri TV, Panasonic Center (a showroom for the latest Panasonic products), the Sumitomo Life Insurance Headquarters building, Hotel New Otani Osaka, and other important companies and businesses are situated here, and the atmosphere of the area makes for pleasant walks. There are also a few nice restaurants in the Matsushita IMP Building.

➤ Access: Directly accessible from Osaka Business Park Station (Nagahori Tsurumi-ryokuchi Subway Line), a 7–10 min. walk south from Kyobashi Station (JR Osaka Loop Line, JR Tozai Line, JR Gakkentoshi Line / Katamachi Line, Nagahori Tsurumi-ryokuchi Subway Line, Keihan lines), and a 5 min. walk southeast from Osakajokitazume Station (JR Tozai Line).

➤ Japanese Address: 大阪市中央区城見 1-2-27 (Crystal Tower)

Tennoji / East Osaka City Sightseeing Guide

Overview

Tennoji and eastern Osaka City provide a diverse mix of multiculturalism, retro and historical sites, shopping and entertainment, natural spaces, and many of Osaka City's most important temples and shrines, including the first official Buddhist temple established in Japan, Shitennoji Temple. Some of the city's most unique and least-known spots can be discovered here. (Also see the essay on p. 194, "In Defense of Shin-Imamiya, Shinsekai and Nishinari.")

Shinsekai

■ Spa World (スパワールド)

Rating: 4

Despite being located in a rather run-down part of the city, this unique, 24-hour facility has a lot to offer, including a full *onsen* (hot spring) experience without having to leave town. There are various indoor and outdoor baths with Asian and European themes (separated by gender), a swimming pool with water slides so the whole family can have fun together, saunas, a stone spa, resting areas and hotel rooms, a gym, massage and beauty services, and entertainment and dining facilities. The natural *onsen* baths are supplied with real hot spring water pumped up from deep within the earth. Not only do you get to visit various internationally themed baths with one ticket, you can enjoy a genuine Japanese hot spring experience without having leave Osaka City!

- ➤ Access: Directly outside exit 5 of Dobutsuen-mae Station (Midosuji and Sakaisuji Subway Lines), or 3–7 min. walk from Shin-Imamiya Station (JR lines, Nankai lines) and Minamikasumicho Station (Hankai Streetcar Line)

- ➤ Cost: Use of the facilities for 3 hours during the day costs 2,400 yen on weekdays and 2,700 yen on weekends and public holidays. All-day use (10:00 AM to midnight) costs 2,700 yen on weekdays and 3,000 yen on weekends and public holidays. Children's admission costs less. Hotel rooms and certain services incur additional charges. Please refer the prices section of Spa World's website (see below) for more details, and also for special deals and coupons during certain times of the year.

- ➤ Open: Generally open 24 hours a day, 365 days a year, except when it is closed on occasion for legally required inspections.

- ➤ Phone: 06-6631-0001

- ➤ Additional Information: http://www.spaworld.co.jp/english

- ➤ Japanese Address: 大阪市浪速区恵美須東 3-4-24

■ Tsutentaku and Shinsekai (通天閣・新世界)

Rating: 4

In the early twentieth century, Shinsekai (lit. "new world") was the newest entertainment district in Osaka, with modern technology such as aerial lifts, neon lights, and streetcars clanging up and down the nearby boulevards. While it has lost some of that glamorous feel, Tsutenkaku tower as well as many old shops and eating establishments remain, keeping the retro spirit of old Osaka alive to this day. Shinsekai was originally built to resemble New York City on one half and Paris on the other, with Tsutenkaku ("Tower to the Heavens") as its shining centerpiece. The tower was first built in 1912, modeled closely after the Eiffel Tower, and rebuilt again in 1956 after being scrapped during World War II for materials. It was thanks to local donations and neighborhood organization efforts that this tower was rebuilt, as people in Osaka, and especially those in the Shinsekai area, saw it as a piece of local history and an invaluable part of the city's character.

Today's Tsutenkaku is slightly different in shape than the original while still retaining the original feel, and the current incarnation is illuminated spectacularly at night by Hitachi lighting. It stands at 103 meters (approximately 430 feet), which is not extraordinarily tall but still affords a stunning view of most of Osaka City and the sunset over the bay. As for the old streetcars of Shinsekai, Hankai Tramway operates the last two remaining lines in Osaka, one of which still runs in front of Tsutenkaku and stops near Shinsekai's northern and southern entrances.

Shinsekai today is also famous for its affordable and delicious dining, concentrated in the lively Jan Jan Yokocho alley where *kushikatsu* (various fried foods on skewers) can be eaten. Unlike many *kushikatsu* establishments, shops in Shinsekai are very careful about which oils they use for cooking, which is why the neighborhood's cuisine so outstandingly delicious. Shinsekai is also the best place to go for *fugu* (blowfish) cuisine in Osaka.

Tsutenkaku is one of the three most symbolic sights of Osaka (the others being the Glico running man in Dotombori (see p. 49) and Osaka Castle (see p. 94)), and Shinsekai is a unique neighborhood you won't find anywhere else in Japan. By all means, make these part of your Osaka itinerary.

➢ Access: The most convenient entrance to Shinsekai is right in front of exit 3 of Ebisucho Station on the Sakaisuji Subway Line, and across the street from Ebisucho Station on the Hankai Streetcar Line. Tsutenkaku is right in the middle of Shinsekai, and Jan Jan Yokocho extends south from there until Spa World (see p. 102). You can also get off at Dobutsuen-mae Station (Midosuji and Sakaisuji Subway Lines), Shin-Imamiya Station (JR lines, Nankai lines) or Minamikasumicho Station (Hankai Streetcar Line) and enter from behind Spa World.

➢ Cost: Tsutenkaku costs 600 yen for adults, 500 yen for university students, 400 yen for middle and high school students, 300 yen for children younger than that, and 400 yen for handicapped guests. Group discounts are available.

➢ Open: Tsutenkaku is open every day of the year from 9:00 AM to 9:00 PM (last admission at 8:30 PM).

➢ Phone: 06-6641-9555

> ➤ Additional Information: http://www.tsutenkaku.co.jp/Guide -pdf/English.pdf (Tsutenkaku pamphlet in PDF format), http://www.shinsekai.ne.jp/en (Shinsekai's website)

> ➤ Japanese Address (Tsutenkaku): 大阪市浪速区恵美須東 1-18-6

Tsuruhashi/Tamatsukuri/Uehonmachi

■ Tsuruhashi (鶴橋)

Rating: 3

This area of Osaka is populated by many Koreans and Japanese-Koreans (immigrants and family members of past immigrants), and as a result it is home to a large number of unique shops selling traditional Korean apparel, sweets and other goods. In a word, it is Osaka's own "Korea Town." But the main attraction is the food: not only is there a large number of fish and vegetable markets, there are countless delicious, reasonably priced restaurants serving popular Korean dishes. When you walk into the shopping arcades of Tsutentaku, your senses will be treated to a barrage of smells, sights and sounds as you wander through the almost unbelievably cramped passageways between shops and buildings. I recommend taking at least one meal here, or at least purchasing some scrumptious *chijimi* (also known as *pajeon* in Korean) from a street vendor.

> ➤ Access: Just outside Tsuruhashi Station on the Kintetsu lines, JR Osaka Loop Line, and Sennichimae Subway Line.

■ Osaka Shinkabukiza (大阪新歌舞伎座)

Rating: 2

(See p. 58)

■ Ikutama Shrine (生國魂神社)

Rating: 1

Ikutama Shrine, referred to as "Ikutama-san" by locals and sometimes by its older name, "Naniwa Oyashiro," has a history dating back to ancient times—it is even mentioned in the *Nihon Shoki*, one of the oldest historical records of Japan. The shrine was relocated to its current location in the sixteenth century in response to an order by Toyotomi Hideyoshi, to make room for the construction of Osaka Castle (see p. 94). Its wooden *honden* (main hall) is a modern reconstruction, but it still possesses the elegant austerity of the classic Shinto architectural style—in fact, the *Ikutama-zukuri* architectural style is based on this very building. Be sure to follow the path around the side of the main hall to see smaller "branches" of other shrines from around Japan, as well as the surprisingly massive carp swimming near one of the orange gates. Tojiji Temple is also nearby (see p. 108).

> ➤ Access: 5 min. walk from exit 3 of Tanimachi 9-chome Station on the Sennichimae and Tanimachi Subway Lines, or a 10 min. walk from Osaka-Uehommachi Station on the Kintetsu lines. From Tanimachi 9-chome Station, walk straight (south) after leaving exit 3, turn right at the second street you pass, and continue straight until you see the shrine's gate. From Osaka-Uehommachi Station, follow the underground corridors connecting to Tanimachi 9-chome Station, and then take exit 3 and follow the same directions.

> ➤ Open: Normally open from 9:00 AM to 5:00 PM, but hours vary depending on the season and shrine events.

> ➤ Phone: 06-6771-0002

> ➤ Japanese Address: 大阪市天王寺区生玉町 13-9

■ Sanko Shrine (三光神社)

Rating: 1

This shrine is famous because of its location at the end of a tunnel that is said to have once led to Osaka Castle. It was dug under the supervision of Sanada Yukimura, a samurai vassal of the Toyotomi family—a family whose base of military power was in Osaka, and who ruled Japan until power was usurped by the Tokugawa in the early seventeenth century. The Toyotomi resisted until 1615, when they and their allies lost during the second siege of Osaka Castle by the Tokugawa and their allies, leading to the demise of the Toyotomi.

Sanada played a vital role in the battle against the Tokugawa alliance, although he eventually died in battle. Osaka has always had a sense of independence and resistance to influence from Edo/Tokyo, a sentiment that remains to this day in certain ways. The statue of Sanada Yukimura at Sanko Shrine is not only a testament to this heroic figure's important historical role and contributions, but to the autonomy and local pride of Osakans throughout the city's long history.

➢ Access: 3 min. walk from Tamatsukuri Station on the Nagahori Tsurumi-ryokuchi Subway Line, and 8–10 min. walk from Tamatsukuri Station on the JR Osaka Loop Line. If you are taking the subway, take exit 2, turn left after reaching ground level and walk straight (about two blocks) until you see the shrine on your right. From the JR line, the best method is to take exit 1 and walk west (crossing a boulevard and many small streets along the way) until you see what looks like a park, inside of which is the shrine. If you are walking from the JR station, check the map inside the station before setting out to get an idea of your route.

➢ Phone: 06-6761-0372

➢ Japanese Address: 大阪市天王寺区玉造本町 14-90

■ Tamatsukuri Inari Shrine (玉造稲荷神社)

Rating: 1

Although originally constructed in the year 12 BC and thought to have been visited by the famed Prince Shotoku (also see Eifukuji Temple on p. 129), Tamatsukuri Inari Shrine was abandoned for a long period of time before being rebuilt under the direction of Toyotomi Hideyori (son of the great unifier Toyotomi Hideyoshi) in 1603 AD. It was further rebuilt and has been renamed many times since, and the current shrine buildings date back to 1954. There is an unusual stone *torii* gate located on the shrine grounds: this was originally donated by Toyotomi Hideyori at the time of the 1603 reconstruction, and the bottom half of the gate is missing because it crumbled during the massive Hanshin-Awaji Earthquake in 1995, leaving the heavier upper portion intact. Inari, a commonly seen

Shinto fox deity connected with rice and agriculture, was enshrined here by Toyotomi Hideyoshi in the late sixteenth century to protect Osaka Castle. "Love fox" (恋キツネ) charms are also sold here— these are carved in the shape of the *kitsune* fox, a common symbol of Inari (see photograph on p. 17).

➢ Access: 5–7 min. walk from Tamatsukuri Station (Nagahori Tsurumi-ryokuchi Subway Line, JR Osaka Loop Line) and Morinomiya Station (Chuo and Nagahori Tsurumi-ryokuchi Subway Lines, JR Osaka Loop Line). If possible, check the map inside the station before heading out, because the shrine is buried inside a network of small, somewhat confusing streets. You can also show the name of the shrine (the Japanese version in the header above) to passersby and ask for directions if you get lost.

➢ Phone: 06-6941-3821

➢ Japanese Address: 大阪市中央区玉造 2-3-8

■ Tojiji Temple (藤次寺)

Rating: 1

Tojiji was originally built in the early ninth century, in connection with the Fujiwara family. After its destruction during the allied bombings in 1945, it was rebuilt at its current location. This lovely little temple is hidden away just off of Tanimachi-suji Blvd. and filled with greenery, and its resting area offers a good place to take a quick breather between visits to other sightseeing spots nearby. The plum blossoms on the temple grounds bloom in the winter, creating a lovely spectacle. Ikutama Shrine is located nearby (see p. 105).

➢ Access: 1 min. walk from exit 3 of Tanimachi 9-chome Station on the Sennichimae and Tanimachi Subway Lines, or a 5 min. walk from Osaka-Uehommachi Station on the Kintetsu lines. From Tanimachi 9-chome Station, take exit 3, and after reaching ground level walk straight and you will immediately see the small entrance to Tojiji Temple on your right. From Osaka-Uehommachi Station, follow the underground passages connecting to Tanimachi 9-chome Station, and then take exit 3 and follow the same directions as above.

➤ Phone: 06-6771-8144

➤ Japanese Address: 大阪市天王寺区生玉町 1-6

Tennoji

■ Shitennoji Temple (四天王寺)

Rating: 3

Shitennoji Temple was, in a way, the official starting point for Buddhism in Japan, and it is the central point for the religion in Osaka. This temple has also been known by the names Arahakaji, Nanbaji, and Mitsuji. The oldest government-administered Buddhist temple in Japan, Shitennoji is said to have been built by Prince Shotoku (Shotoku Taishi) in 593. Prince Shotoku was an avid believer in Buddhism before it had spread to Japan, and he allegedly played a leading role in importing from China this religion that is ubiquitous in Japan today. "Shitenno" means "four heavenly kings," to whom Prince Shotoku prayed for the victory of his Soga Clan over his enemies (the Monobe Clan) in a war with the goal of establishing the new religion in Japan. (For the site of Prince Shotoku's mausoleum, see p. 129.)

The temple has a beautiful main gate and an elegant five-storey pagoda. Shitennoji has undergone repeated reconstructions—the most recent in 1963—but its architectural layout has remained unchanged. The area was once a center of Buddhist power large enough to threaten and even go to war against the government/ imperial court, and the old neighborhood surrounding Shitennoji is still full of temples today. In addition, the area is famous for its numerous small shops selling exceptionally delicious *tsukemono* (pickled vegetables).

A large-scale flea market is held here on the 21st of each month, and the famous Doya Doya Festival (see p. 175) is held here every year.

- ➤ Access: 5 min. walk from Shitennoji-Yuhigaoka Station on the Tanimachi Subway Line (take exit 4 and walk southeast), or 15 min. walk from Tennoji Station (JR lines, Tanimachi and Midosuji Subway Lines) and Osaka-Abenobashi Station (Kintetsu Minami-Osaka Line)—walk north along Tanimachi-suji, the main north–south boulevard passing in front of both stations.

- ➤ Cost: Entry to the main temple building costs 300 yen for adults, costs 200 yen for college and high school students, and is free for visitors age 15 or younger. The treasure hall costs 200 yen for adults, costs 100 yen for college and high school students, and is free for visitors age 15 or younger. You can explore the rest of the expansive temple grounds for free.

- ➤ Open: 8:30 AM to 4:30 PM from April to September, 8:30 AM to 4:00 PM from October to March (last admission is 30 min. before closing time). The treasure hall is closed on Mondays (but open if Monday is a public holiday).

- ➤ Phone: 06-6771-0066

- ➤ Japanese Address: 大阪市天王寺区四天王寺 1-11-18

■ Tennoji/Abenobashi (天王寺・阿倍野橋)

Rating: 2

As one of the largest transportation hubs in Osaka, the area around Tennoji and Osaka-Abenobashi Stations is, unsurprisingly, bustling and full of life. It is steadily developing into a significant competitor with Kita and Minami in terms of shopping, with the Kintetsu Department Store, the upscale Hoop shopping mall tucked away in the backstreets, Tennoji Mio attached directly to JR Tennoji Station, the massive new Abeno Market Park Q's Mall, and plenty of underground shops and small, local stores.

However, the main attraction of the area is the expansive Tennoji Park, which includes the Tennoji Zoo, Keitakuen Garden (which once belonged to the wealthy Sumitomo family) and the Osaka City Museum of Fine Arts. There are also numerous good restaurants and bars in the area (Tin's Hall is a particularly popular bar among expats, and it often hosts live music). All of these sites are all within reasonable walking distance of Shitennoji Temple (see p. 109), Isshinji Temple (see next entry) and other temples and shrines.

➢ Access: Tennoji Station (Midosuji and Tanimachi Subway Lines, JR lines), Osaka-Abenobashi Station (Kintetsu Minami-Osaka Line), and Tennoji-ekimae Station (Hankai Uemachi Streetcar Line). Tennoji Park is a 3–5 min. walk from the stations.

➢ Cost: Tennoji Park has an entrance fee of 150 yen per person. The Tennoji Zoo costs an additional 500 yen per person, and the Osaka City Museum of Fine Arts costs 300 yen for adults (200 yen for college and high school students, free for visitors younger than that).

➢ Open: Tennoji Park and facilities within are open from 9:30 AM until 5:00 PM (open until 8:00 PM on some weekends and public holidays). The park is closed on Mondays (or the next day if Monday is a public holiday). Hoop is open from 11:00 AM to 9:00 PM (restaurants are open until 11:00 PM; some shops have different business hours). Tennoji Mio is open from 11:00 AM to 9:00 PM (restaurants are open until 10:00 PM; some shops have different business hours). The Kintetsu Department Store is open from 10:30 AM to 8:00 PM (later during the holiday season), and its restaurants are open until 10:00 PM. Most facilities in Abeno Market Park Q's Mall are open from 10:00 AM to 9:00 PM, although hours vary by shop.

➢ Phone: 06-6771-8401 (Tennoji Park), 06-6624-1111 (Kintetsu Department Store), 06-6626-2500 (Hoop), 06-6770-1000 (Tennoji Mio), 06-6556-7000 (Abeno Market Park Q's Mall)

➢ Additional Information: http://www.osaka-art-museum.jp /english/index.html (Osaka City Museum of Fine Arts), http://www.d-kintetsu.co.jp/store/abeno/foreigner/index.html (Kintetsu Department Store)

➢ Japanese Address: Most places mentioned are a short walk from the train stations listed in the "Access" section above. Hoop's address is 大阪市阿倍野区阿倍野筋 1-2-30, and Tin's Hall's address is 大阪市天王寺区南河堀町 10-3.

■ Isshinji Temple (一心寺)

Rating: 1

Although you wouldn't know it from Isshinji's main gate, which is an interesting mix of modern art and traditional Buddhist architecture, this temple was originally built in 1185. The gate was designed by the current head priest, who is also an architect. Isshinji is particularly known for its "bone Buddha" statues, which are Buddhist images made from bones of the deceased; this practice began here in 1851, when tens of thousands of bones were collected to make the first statue, and since 1887 a statue has been made every ten years. This temple is on the way if you are walking between Den Den Town (see p. 62) and the Tennoji/Abenobashi area (see previous entry) or Shitennoji Temple (see p. 109).

➢ Access: The temple is located at the back side of Tennoji Park (see previous entry), a 7–10 min. walk from Ebisucho Station. It can also be reached in 10–15 min. on foot from Tennoji Station (Tanimachi and Midosuji Subway Lines, JR lines), Osaka-Abenobashi Station (Kintetsu Minami-Osaka Line), Tennoji-ekimae Station (Hankai Streetcar Line), and Shitennoji-mae Yuhigaoka Station (Tanimachi Subway Line). From Ebisucho Station, which provides the easiest access, take exit 3, walk east toward the elevated expressway, pass underneath and keep going straight along that boulevard until you see Isshinji Temple on your right (you will have to do a bit of uphill walking).

➢ Open: The gates are open from 5:00 AM to 6:00 PM.

➢ Phone: 06-6771-0444

➢ Japanese Address: 大阪市天王寺区逢阪 2-8-69

Farther East

■ Tsurumi Ryokuchi Park (花博記念公園鶴見緑地)

Rating: 2

There are many different sides to this diverse and fascinating park. It was home to the 1990 International Garden and Greenery Exposition, and a large number of countries built structures and gardens on the park grounds to represent their national cultures. The park was designed to display flowers in bloom during all four seasons of the year, and a wide variety of animal and bird species lives within the grounds. In addition, there is a fascinating flower conservatory (Sakuya Konohana Kan), sports facilities, a rose garden with a Japanese tea house, and a picturesque windmill on a hill from which you can look out over the surrounding suburbs.

Tsurumi Ryokuchi Park is a superb place to relax and take a long walk among refreshing natural scenery and blooming flowers. On Sundays, you can enjoy watching elderly men and women dance and sing *enka* (classic popular songs) along the walking paths using portable karaoke equipment, which is more than a little entertaining.

➤ Access: The main entrance is a 5 min. walk from Tsurumi-ryokuchi Station on the Nagahori Tsurumi-ryokuchi Subway Line. The path to the park is easy to understand once you exit the station (there is only one exit).

➤ Cost: There is no park entrance fee. The flower conservatory, Sakuya Konohana Kan, costs 500 yen (group discounts are available).

➤ Open: Sakuya Konohana Kan is open from 10:00 AM to 5:00 PM (last admission at 4:30 PM), and it is closed on Mondays (or the next day if Monday is a public holiday) and during the New Year's holiday period.

➤ Phone: 06-6912-0650 (park office), 06-6912-0055 (Sakuya Konohana Kan)

➤ Japanese Address: 大阪巿鶴見区緑地公園 2-163 (Sakuya Konohana Kan)

■ **Yodogawa Lagoons / Shirokita Park (淀川ワンド群・城北公園)**

Rating: 1

The term for this type of body of water is *wando* in Japanese, a word whose origins are unclear but are said by some to come from the Ainu language of the native Ainu people of Hokkaido (Japan's northernmost prefecture). In English, *wando* is often translated as [riverine] lagoon or riverside pool, so I chose "lagoon" for simplicity's sake.

The Yodogawa lagoons are well-preserved aquatic habitats for a number of fish, insects, and other creatures, and they provide a refreshing natural spot amidst the concrete grays of eastern Osaka. The peaceful, vibrant green islands and silently standing pools are surrounded on all sides by the rushing force of the Yodogawa River. There are plenty of spots near the riverbank in nearby Shirokita Park for a sunny picnic, and a spectacular view of the lagoons from above with the central city's distant skyline as a backdrop can be enjoyed from the sidewalk of the massive bridge cutting across the river.

➤ Access: The best way to get here is to take bus 34, 110 or 110A (bound for Moriguchi Shako-mae) and get off at Shirokitakoen-mae bus stop, which will put you right in front of the park and near the river. Bus 34 leaves from Osaka Station / Umeda Station, bus 110 leaves from Temmabashi Station (Tanimachi Subway Line, Keihan lines), and bus 100A leaves from Miyakojima Station (Tanimachi Subway Line). You can also take the subway to Taishibashi-Imaichi Station (Tanimachi and Imazato Subway Lines), and walk west from exit 5 or 6 for 10–15 min. until you reach the park (you will be walking parallel to the river, which is about 5 min. to your north).

➤ Phone: 6-6928-0005 (Shirokita Park office)

➤ Japanese Address: 大阪市旭区生江 3-29-1

West Osaka City / Bay Area Sightseeing Guide

Overview

Osaka has long had deep ties with the sea, and Osaka Bay is a defining part of the city's culture. Since ancient times, international trade and cultural exchange through Osaka's ports have sustained it and helped it grow into the city it is today. Aside from a wide selection of shopping and entertainment, the waterfront area has one of Japan's best aquariums, Universal Studios Japan, a giant Ferris wheel, a massive UFO-shaped stadium, a maritime museum, and even Japan's smallest "mountain" reaching a height of 4.53 meters (15 feet)!

Bay Area

■ Osaka Aquarium Kaiyukan (海遊館)

Rating: 5

This aquarium is the highlight of the bay area and one of the best aquariums in Japan. It has two huge whale sharks as well as some other rare and interesting aquatic creatures, including the creepy, alien-like spider crabs. Its exhibit layout is innovative: the ten-storey whale shark tank extends vertically through the center of the building, and guests start from the top and spiral their way downward around this tank, viewing other exhibits while catching glimpses of the whale sharks from various angles. Voice guidance systems and English-speaking staff are available. The Aquarium holds events such as the "Penguin Parade" and a Christmas lights display (see p. 179) in December every year, the *Santa Maria* bay sightseeing ship (see p. 119) departs from behind the building, and the Tempozan Giant Ferris Wheel and Tempozan Marketplace (see p. 117) are just a few steps away.

➢ Access: 5–7 min. walk from Osakako Station on the Chuo Subway Line. Take exit 1, walk straight after you have descended to ground level continue straight ahead until you reach the first major intersection (first traffic light), turn left and go straight until you reach a T-intersection with another boulevard, then turn right and walk straight until you reach the aquarium (it will be on your left). You can also follow the directions for the Tempozan Giant Ferris Wheel and Tempozan Marketplace (see p. 117) and turn left at the final location.

➢ Cost: 2,000 yen for adults, 900 yen for children and 400 yen for infants. Group discounts and annual passes are available.

➢ Open: 10:00 AM to 8:00 PM (last admission at 7:30 PM). Closed on specific days, which vary by season (see website below).

➢ Phone: 06-6576-5501

➢ Additional Information: http://www.kaiyukan.com/language/eng /index.htm

➢ Japanese Address: 大阪市港区海岸通 1 丁目

■ **Universal Studios Japan (ユニバーサル・スタジオ・ジャパン)**

Rating: 5

Universal Studios Japan, known colloquially as USJ, is almost an exact replica of Hollywood's Universal Studios, but with far more people and longer lines. Like the American incarnation, it has an attached shopping mall area, complete with a Hard Rock Cafe. The park itself is identical to its Hollywood counterpart, with thrilling rides based on popular movies as well as shopping and other facilities throughout nine distinct zones. There are seasonal events for Halloween, Christmas and other holidays throughout the year. Additionally, USJ's convenient central-city location and good train access are big advantages (you can even access it by ferry from other parts of the bay), and there are various hotels nearby if you want to stay right next to the park.

➤ Access: 5 min. walk from Universal-city Station on the JR Yumesaki Line (also known as the JR Sakurajima Line). Through services operate from Osaka Station and other parts of Osaka, running along the JR Osaka Loop Line and then continuing to USJ from Nishikujo Station. If you are coming from the Namba area, take the Hanshin Namba Line to Nishikujo Station and transfer to the JR line from there.

➤ Cost: A 1-day pass is 6,200 yen for adults and 4,100 yen for children, a 2-day pass is 10,700 yen / 7,200 yen, and a "Twilight & Day Pass" is 8,200 yen / 6,100 yen. Passes include admission to all attractions.

➤ Open: Hours vary based on season and event schedules. Refer to the website for more information (see below).

➤ Phone: 06-6465-3000

➤ Additional Information: http://www.usj.co.jp/e

➤ Japanese Address: 大阪市此花区桜島 2-1-33

■ Tempozan Giant Ferris Wheel and Tempozan Marketplace (天保山大観覧車・天保山マーケットプレイス)

Rating: 3

The Tempozan Giant Ferris Wheel is one of Osaka City's two giant Ferris wheels (also see p. 75). Unlike the HEP FIVE Ferris wheel, the Tempozan wheel offers a view of the bay and Osaka's neighboring cities, rather than central Osaka City—you can see as far as the Akashi Kaikyo Bridge and Kansai International Airport on clear days. It reaches a height of 112.5 meters (369 feet), and one ride takes about 15 minutes. The Ferris wheel is directly connected to the Tempozan Marketplace, a facility with shopping, entertainment, restaurants, a concert hall and more.

Although the giant Ferris wheel in Rinku Town (see p. 144) offers a more stunning bay view, this one is nearly as impressive, and its location near other sights such as the aquarium (see p. 115) is a big advantage.

➢ Access: 5 min. walk from Osakako Station on the Chuo Subway Line. From exit 2, walk straight until you reach the second traffic light, from which you can easily see the Ferris wheel.

➢ Cost: 700 yen for all guests 3 years or older. Group discounts are available.

➢ Open: 10:00 AM to 10:00 PM (last boarding at 9:30 PM)

➢ Phone: 06-6576-6222

➢ Japanese Address: 大阪市港区海岸通 1-1-10

■ Osaka Maritime Museum (大阪市立海洋館 なにわの海の館)

Rating: 2

Osaka has been an important base of maritime trade throughout its long history, and this museum was established to commemorate that history and educate and entertain visitors. The dome-shaped structure was built in the Nanko port area on a basin jutting out into the sea in order to give it the appearance of floating on water, and the museum is accessed by an underwater tunnel. Exhibits and facilities include a 3D film theater (Theater of the Sea), multimedia exhibits (including the Sea Adventure Pavilion theater) on the development of sea trade in Osaka and around the world, a seventeenth-century trade ship replica called the *Naniwa Maru*, a yacht simulator, and artifacts and woodblock prints related to Osaka's maritime past.

➢ Access: 5 min. walk from Cosmosquare Station on the Chuo Subway Line and Nanko Port Town Line / New Tram Line.

➢ Cost: Museum admission is 600 yen for adults and free for children (middle school students or younger) and senior citizens (age 65 or older). Theater of the Sea and the Sea Adventure Pavilion are 400 yen for adults and 200 yen for children (admission fees must be paid separately for both facilities). The Yacht Simulator is 300 yen per ride.

➢ Open: 10:00 AM to 5:00 PM, closed on Mondays (or the following day if Monday is a public holiday) and during the New Year's holiday period.

➢ Phone: 06-4703-2900

➢ Additional Information: http://www.jikukan-ogbc.jp/english /index.html

➢ Japanese Address: 大阪市住之江区南港北 2-5-20

■ *Santa Maria* Bay Cruise (サンタマリア 遊覧船)

Rating: 2

The *Santa Maria* is a replica of the ship used by Christopher Columbus when he discovered America, although it is twice the size of the original. This sightseeing boat takes passengers on cruises around Osaka Bay. It is one of the Aqua Bus tours (see p. 51 for more details).

■ The Asia & Pacific Trade Center (ATC) (アジア太平洋 トレードセンター(ATC))

Rating: 1

The Asia & Pacific Trade Center (ATC) is located in the Nanko port area on Sakishima, an artificial island in Osaka Bay. Before the economic crash in the early 1990s, this area was developing rapidly, on track to become a rival to Tokyo's Odaiba district. However, the island is still a central focus of urban redevelopment, especially with recent planning initiatives and the relocation of certain government offices there. The commercial center of Nanko is ATC, a large complex that hosts shops, offices, and other commercial and trade-related facilities.

ATC is located near Osaka's international ferry terminal and bonded trade area, and it was originally part of the city's attempt to create a novel, forward-looking international trade zone. ATC houses two major facilities: International Trade Mart (ITM), where you can buy imported and domestic goods, and O's, which is a facility containing various restaurants. There are also event facilities inside ATC. Although this trade center does not come close to being one of the top shopping spots in Osaka City, its peaceful bayside location and occasional events make it worth a look. It's also good if you are near the aquarium (see p. 51) and looking for a place to eat afterward. Also check out the nearby Cosmo Tower (see next entry).

> Access: Connected directly to exit 2 of Trade Center-mae Station (Nanko Port Town Line / New Tram Line).

> Open: Most shops are open from 10:00 AM to 8:00 PM, and most restaurants from 10:00 AM to 10:00 PM.

> Phone: 06-6615-5230

> Additional Information: http://www.atc-co.com/pdf/atc_eng.pdf

> Japanese Address: 大阪市住之江区南港北 2-1-10

■ Cosmo Tower (コスモタワー)

Rating: 1

Developed on the artificial island of Sakishima in Osaka Bay, and following the same development plan behind the construction of ATC (see previous entry) for creating a new international trade and commerce zone, Cosmo Tower (formerly known as the Osaka World Trade Center Building) is tied with the Rinku Gate Building in Rinku Town (see p. 144) as the second tallest building in Japan. The 52nd floor of this 55-storey, 256-meter (840-foot) building offers a sweeping view of the bay area and sights across the water such as Kansai International Airport, Kobe City, Mount Rokko in Hyogo Prefecture, and on clear days, Awaji Island. The view from Cosmo Tower is best at night, when you can admire the sunset followed by illumination of the buildings surrounding Osaka Bay. Cosmo Tower has event facilities for musical performances and other events, and the observatory sometimes hosts live jazz music. There are also restaurant and amusement facilities inside.

> Access: Connected to exit 1 of Trade Center-mae Station (Nanko Port Town Line / New Tram Line).

> Cost: The observatory costs 500 yen for adults (high school students or older), 200 for students younger than that, and 400

yen for senior citizens (age 70 or older). Group discounts are available.

➤ Open: The observatory is open year-round, from 1:00 PM to 10:00 PM on weekdays, and from 11:00 AM to 10:00 PM on weekends (last admission is 30 min. before closing).

➤ Phone: 06-6615-6055

➤ Japanese Address: 大阪市住之江区南港北 1-14-16

■ Mount Tempozan (天保山)

Rating: 1

Even though it is officially recognized as a mountain, Mount Tempozan's summit only reaches a height of 4.53 meters (15 feet), making it is Japan's smallest mountain. An artificial slope built in 1831, the original height of Tempozan was approximately 20 meters (66 feet), and it was used as a navigational landmark for ships coming into the busy trading port. It is currently located within Tempozan Park, which actually has hills higher than the mountain's summit itself. If you climb to the top, the Mount Tempozan Expedition Society, based out of a cafe called Yamagoya (near the station), will issue you a certificate verifying your feat for a 100 yen fee.

➤ Access: Mount Tempozan is a 10 min. walk from exit 2 of Osakako Station (Chuo Subway Line). From exit 2, walk straight until you reach the second traffic light, then turn right and walk until you reach the park. The ascent to the summit can be made in approx. 1 min. To get the headquarters of the Tempozan Expedition Society in cafe Yamagoya, walk straight from exit 4 of Osakako Station, turn left at the first corner (next to the Family Mart convenience store), turn right at the next corner after that, and walk straight, looking for Yamagoya (山小屋) on your right side (it's before the next intersection).

➤ Additional Information: http://www5.ocn.ne.jp/~tenpo45 (the Tempozan Expedition Society's (天保山山岳会) website, in Japanese only)

➤ Japanese Address: 大阪市港区築港 3-2

West-Central

■ Kujo Neighborhood (九条地区)

Rating: 2

This is by no means a fashionable or trendy part of town, and vestiges of its past industrial character still remain. Hanshin Electric Railway opened a train line in 2009 that passes through this area, directly connecting it with Namba and western bedroom towns such as Amagasaki and Nishinomiya. It's an old residential neighborhood, and there are number of narrow streets with long wooden houses, charming cafes, and restaurants to explore. One of the great things about large Japanese cities like Osaka is that, behind all the lights and glamour, there are quiet urban neighborhoods like this where people still know each other's names, and this local feel is the main appeal of the Kujo neighborhood. If you want to be blown away, go to Minami (see p. 49); if you want to see a more subdued and traditional side of Osaka that most people miss out on, take a stroll around Kujo.

➤ Access: Kujo Station on the Chuo Subway Line or Hanshin Namba Line.

■ Kyocera Dome Osaka (京セラドーム)

Rating: 2

Kyocera Dome Osaka (referred to as "Osaka Dome" by locals) is a baseball stadium and the home field for the Orix Buffalos, but it is more widely known for hosting Gamba Osaka soccer matches and Hanshin Tigers baseball games. It has a capacity of a little more than 36,000, and its shape is said to resemble a UFO—the exterior architecture of the dome alone makes it worth a visit. Besides sporting events, world-class musical performers from the United States and other countries also hold concerts here. Tours of the stadium can be taken for 1,000 for adults and 500 yen for children (advance reservation required).

➤ Access: 2–3 min. on foot from Dome-mae Station (Hanshin Namba Line) and Dome-mae Chiyozaki Station (Nagahori

Tsurumi-ryokuchi Subway Line). About 5 min. northwest on foot from Taisho Station (JR Osaka Loop Line, Nagahori Tsurumi-ryokuchi Subway Line).

➤ Phone: 06-6586-0106

➤ Japanese Address: 大阪市西区千代崎 3-2-1

South Osaka City Sightseeing Guide

Overview

South Osaka City has its own unique history and culture. It is home to Sumiyoshi Grand Shrine, one of the Kansai region's most important shrines, as well as Imamiya-Ebisu Shrine, the main stage for one of Japan's largest New Year's festivals, Toka Ebisu (see p. 175). Even though sightseeing attractions are scarce, south Osaka has a gritty kind of charm that many residents take pride in— including this author, who spent a considerable amount of time living there. (Also see the essay on p. 194, "In Defense of Shin-Imamiya, Shinsekai and Nishinari.")

Sightseeing

■ Sumiyoshi Grand Shrine (住吉大社)

Rating: 5

Temples and shrines are not the type of attraction Osaka City is famous for, mostly because it is overshadowed by the popularity of nearby destinations like Kyoto and Nara, but Osaka's Sumiyoshi Shrine is one of the finest Shinto shrines in the Kansai region. This particular shrine is the head Sumiyoshi shrine in Japan (there are thousands across the country), and its deities offer protection for the nation, support in warfare and help for *waka* poets. It has beautiful buildings that predate the introduction of Buddhism to Japan, a development that resulted in the mixing of Buddhist and Shinto architectural styles and ultimately the decline of the Shinto style.

Besides displaying superb examples of the *sumiyoshi-zukuri* architectural style in old buildings with elegant thatched roofs, the shrine also features a *torii* gate that is shaped differently than that of other shrines and a stunning *taikobashi* arch bridge. Sumiyoshi Grand Shrine also appeared in *The Tale of Genji* (a famous work of Japanese literature that is considered to be the world's first novel), and at that time it faced the sea and was known for its beautiful beach, although it is landlocked today. Additionally, the shrine was patronized by the imperial family starting in the tenth century.

Today, Sumiyoshi Grand Shrine's picturesque, high-arching bridge, turtle-filled pond and wooded grounds make for a tranquil and uniquely graceful atmosphere.

➢ Access: Directly in front of Sumiyoshi Torii-mae Station on the Hankai Streetcar Line, or a 3 min. walk east from Sumiyoshitaisha Station on the Nankai main line.

➢ Open: 6:00 AM to 5:00 PM (April to September), 6:30 AM to 5:00 PM (October to February)

➢ Phone: 06-6672-0753

➢ Japanese Address: 大阪市住吉区住吉 2-9-89

■ Imamiya-Ebisu Shrine (今宮戎神社)

Rating: 3 (seasonal)

Imamiya-Ebisu Shrine's history dates back to around the year 600, when a guardian deity was installed here, positioned west of Shitennoji Temple (see p. 109) by Prince Shotoku (Shotoku Taishi). Imamiya-Ebisu enshrines the god Ebisu, who helps those seeking wealth and success in business, so it's no secret that Ebisu is popular even today in the "merchant's capital" of Osaka. The Toka Ebisu Festival (see p. 175), which draws about one million visitors every year, is held at Imamiya-Ebisu Shrine in January.

➢ Access: 5 min. walk from Daikokucho Station (Midosuji and Yotsubashi Subway Lines) and Ebisucho Station (Sakaisuji Subway Line), or 1–2 min. walk from Imamiya-Ebisu Station (Nankai Koya Line, local trains only). It can also be reached in about 10–15 min. on foot (walking south) from Nankai Namba Station (Nankai lines).

- Phone: 06-6643-0150

- Japanese Address: 大阪市浪速区恵美須西 1-6-10

■ Liberty Osaka (Osaka Human Rights Museum) (大阪人権博物館 リバティおおさか)

Rating: 1

This museum was built inside a former elementary school building in Taisho Ward. The exhibits focus on human rights for groups such as women, *burakumin* (a caste of Japanese descended from Edo Period outcast groups assigned to carry out undesirable jobs), foreigners, immigrants (first-generation and beyond), victims of industrial disasters and diseases, AIDS victims, day laborers, and the poor, among others. Exhibits are informative, although sometimes a little dense and hard to follow, and there are complimentary audio guides available in Japanese, English, Chinese and Korean. Volunteers are available to answer questions (in Japanese and sometimes a little English).

This museum was established for a good cause: to help people in the immediate vicinity (Taisho Ward and nearby Nishinari Ward are some of the more neglected parts of Osaka City) and raise general awareness to fight injustice on a larger scale. It is supported by volunteers who generously give their time without expecting compensation.

- Access: 10–15 min. walk from Ashiharabashi Station on the JR Osaka Loop Line. It can also be reached in 5–7 min. on foot from Kizugawa Station on the Nankai Shiomibashi Line, but this old line has very few trains per hour, it stops in a very bad part of town, and it is confusing to walk between the museum and the station, so I recommend using JR (if you do take the Shiomibashi Line, you will need to transfer to Shiomibashi Station from Sakuragawa Station on the Sennichimae Subway Line or Hanshin Namba Line). If you are using JR, take the south exit from Ashiharabashi Station, turn left on the main boulevard and walk straight until your reach a large three-way intersection where the road starts to curve (it has a pedestrian bridge for crossing the road). Turn right on the small street before the big intersection and walk straight until you see the museum on your left.

➢ Cost: 250 yen for adults (500 yen for access to the current special exhibition), 150 yen for middle school and high school students (300 yen for access to the current special exhibition), and free for children (middle school student or younger) and senior citizens (age 65 or older). Admission is free during Human Rights Week (December 4–10).

➢ Open: 10:00 AM to 5:00 PM (last admission at 4:30 PM). Closed on Mondays (or the following day if Monday is a public holiday), every 4th Friday of the month, during the New Year's holiday period, and on museum holidays.

➢ Phone: 06-6561-5891

➢ Additional Information: http://www.liberty.or.jp/topfile /human-top.htm

➢ Japanese Address: 大阪市浪速区浪速西 3-6-36

■ Nagai Park (長居公園)

Rating: 1

Nagai Park hosted the International Association of Athletics Federations 2007 World Championships in Athletics, one of the world's largest track and field competitions, and since that time its popularity among locals has been growing. It is home to the Osaka Museum of Natural History, a stadium, a pool, a horse-riding area, a large botanical garden, and other community and athletics facilities. On weekends, people from all around the neighborhood gather here to sing karaoke, play, take long strolls or just relax in the sun.

➢ Access: Directly outside exit 3 of Nagai Station on the Midosuji Subway Line. 5 min. walk from Nagai Station or Tsurugaoka Station on the JR Hanwa Line.

➢ Cost: The botanical garden costs 200 yen, and a combined ticket can be purchased that also includes admission to the Osaka Museum of Natural History for 300 yen (200 yen for high school and university students). The museum alone costs 300

yen (200 yen for high school and university students). Middle
school students and younger can enter both facilities for free.

- ➤ Open: The botanical garden is open from 9:30 AM to 5:00 PM
  from March to October, and 9:30 AM to 4:30 PM from
  November to February. Last entry is 30 min. before closing time,
  and the garden is closed on Mondays (the next day if Monday is
  a public holiday) and during the New Year's period. Hours for
  the Osaka Museum of Natural History are the same.

- ➤ Phone: 06-6696-7117 (Botanical Garden), 06-6697-6221 (Osaka
  Museum of Natural History)

- ➤ Additional Information: http://www.mus-nh.city.osaka.jp
  /english/index.html (Osaka Museum of Natural History)

- ➤ Japanese Address: 大阪市東住吉区長居公園 1-23

Southern Osaka Prefecture Sightseeing Guide

Overview

Southern Osaka Prefecture is a great place to experience traditional Japan without having to fight crowds as in Nara and Kyoto. A trek south will open your eyes to the traditional townscapes, magnificent temples and shrines, beautiful countryside scenery, colossal imperial tombs and cozy neighborhoods of Osaka Prefecture, so much so that you may just forget you are minutes away from one of the biggest metropolitan centers in the world. The southern part of the prefecture is one of the least-appreciated areas of Osaka, but it is also one of the most culturally rich and fascinating.

Tondabayashi/Kawachinagano/Osakasayama

■ Eifukuji Temple (Prince Shotoku's Mausoleum) (叡福寺)

Rating: 4

Eifukuji Temple is also the location of the mausoleum of Prince Shotoku (Shotoku Taishi), a figure who is credited for importing and spreading Buddhism in Japan (also see Shitennoji Temple on p. 109). The temple belongs to the Shingon sect of Buddhism and was founded in the year 724. In 1574, it was severely damaged by fire during a battle, and in the early seventeenth century it was revived under the supervision of Toyotomi Hideyori (the successor of Toyotomi Hideyoshi) under imperial orders. The Shoryoden building, restored by Hideyori, has been designated as an Important Cultural Property by the Japanese government. The tumulus of Prince Shotoku is just beyond the temple grounds.

Despite the temple's humble entrance gate, visitors will be surprised upon entering to encounter a vast, awe-inspiring temple complex with a massive central hall, a beautiful old pagoda, and numerous other stately structures. This temple complex is usually not very crowded, so you can enjoy exploring it in peace and quiet. I highly recommend combining a stop at Eifukuji with a visit to Tondabayashi's Jinaimachi historic district (see next entry) and Takidani Fudo Myo-oji (see p. 130).

- ➤ Access: From Kishi Station (Kintetsu Nagano Line), ride a Kongo Bus ("Hamuro Mawari Junkan," "Taishi Mawari Junkan," or any bus bound for "Kami no Taishi") and get off at Taishi-mae bus stop (about a 15 min. ride). There are also Kongo Buses to Taishi-mae bus stop from Kaminotaishi Station (Kintetsu Minami-Osaka Line).

- ➤ Open: 9:00 AM to 5:00 PM

- ➤ Phone: 0721-98-0019

- ➤ Japanese Address: 大阪府南河内郡太子町太子 2146

■ Takidani Fudo Myo-oji Temple (瀧谷不動明王寺)

Rating: 4

It is said that this Shingo-sect Buddhist temple got its start when the famed monk Kukai carved three wooden Buddha images in the year 821—the buildings constructed to house them were the first structures of this temple complex. The original temple was built on Mount Takeyama, one kilometer from the current site. Takidani Fudo Myo-oji is particularly popular among those seeking divine assistance related to eye-related ailments or safety when driving.

The temple complex is divided into two separate halves straddling a mountain road—I recommend climbing up both sides. There is a great view of the whole complex from the top of southern side, and a lovely pagoda at the end of a mossy path on the northern side. On the southern side, there is also a hall displaying Buddhist images from the 33 temples of the famous Saigoku pilgrimage route.

- ➤ Access: If you want to go on foot, walk east for 15 min. from Takidanifudo Station on the Kintetsu Nagano Line, following the main road on the south side of the station that crosses over the river (stay on that road the entire way). The road is narrow and busy, with cars that travel fast, no sidewalk, and many blind turns, so be careful while walking. The easiest way to reach the temple, however, is to ask the station attendant about calling a taxi, and also asking for a taxi on the way back at the temple's main office (near the parking lot). On the 28th of every month (the temple's festival day), you can take a Kongo Bus from Tondabayashi Station (Kintetsu Nagano Line) to the final bus stop, Takidanifudo-mae, which is right in front of the temple.

➢ Open: 8:30 AM to 4:00 PM, but hours vary on festival days (the 28th of each month)

➢ Phone: 0721-34-0028

➢ Japanese Address: 大阪府富田林市彼方 1762

■ Tondabayashi Jinaimachi Temple Town (富田林寺内町)

Rating: 4

(See map on p. 207)

This temple town developed after the construction of Koshoji Betsuin Temple in the sixteenth century, which lies at the center. From the seventeenth century onward, the town lost much of its religious character and became a rural trade center. The mansions of wealthy merchants can still be seen today.

The main attraction of Tondabayashi's *jinaimachi* its well-preserved townscape, a stroll through which will make you feel as if you've stepped back more than 400 years in time. Jonomon-suji Street, which is lined on both sides by traditional wooden buildings, is the most picturesque part of the district.

The most impressive residence that can be toured is the Sugiyama Residence, which was built around the same time this temple town was. This massive, two-storey mansion can be explored from end to end, and there are a number of old artifacts on display and impressive woodwork and painted screens to admire. Another lesser-known but beautiful old house is the Katsuma Residence, located on the edge of town near the river. Rather than being organized as a museum, as is the case with the Sugiyama Residence, the Katsuma Residence is still used as a home, and you can view items from the early nineteenth and twentieth centuries inside. There are two nice gardens within its walls that can be admired from the guest room, and there are adorable hand-drawn guidebooks made by children who visited previously, which you can look at while sipping complimentary tea. The small gift shop has some charming souvenirs to take home, as well.

Jinaimachi terra is a small shop/gallery located in the middle of the temple town district, and it carries unique jewelry and other goods that will appeal to female tastes in particular. You can also relax in this shop's living room area and order a glass of fresh fruit juice. The Jinaimachi Cultural Exchange Center provides a place to rest your feet (complete with vending machines and air conditioning, which are welcome if you are sightseeing during the summer) and inquire about directions or other information. The Jinaimachi Center has a few artifacts and pieces of interesting information on display (free of charge). Finally, near Kintetsu Tondabayashi Station, there is a store called Ongashi Tsukasa Katsuraya that sells local souvenir foods. Here you can buy delicious *senbei* rice crackers with images from the *jinaimachi* printed on them as well as various other kinds of cakes and Japanese sweets, any of which make an excellent gift or treat for yourself.

➤ Access: 15 min. walk from Tondabayashi Station (Kintetsu Nagano Line). It takes about 40 min. using a semi-express on the Nagano Line / Minami-Osaka Line from Osaka-Abenobashi Station (next to Tennoji Station) to Tondabayashi Station. From the station, refer to the map on p. 207 for walking directions.

➤ Cost: The Sugiyama Residence costs 400 yen, the Katsura Residence costs 200 yen (includes tea), and entrance to all others facilities mentioned is free.

➤ Open: The Jinaimachi Cultural Exchange Center is open from 10:00 AM to 5:00 PM (closed on Mondays and from December 28 to January 6). Jinaimachi terra is only open on Saturdays and Sundays (except for the last Sunday of the month) from 11:00 AM to 4:00 PM. Koshojo Betsuin Temple is open from 8:30 AM to 5:00 PM daily, but closed some days without notice. The

Sugiyama Residence is open from 10:00 AM to 5:00 PM (until 4:00 PM during winter; closed on Mondays). The Jinaimachi Center is open only on Saturdays and Sundays (except the last Sunday of the month) from 10:00 AM to 5:00 PM (until 4:00 PM during winter). The Katsura Residence is open on Saturdays, Sundays and public holidays from 10:00 AM to 4:00 PM. Onganshi Tsukasa Katsuraya is open every day of the week except Tuesday, from 9:00 AM to 7:00 PM (until 5:00 PM on Sundays and public holidays).

➢ Phone: 0721-26-0110 (Jinaimachi Cultural Exchange Center)

➢ Additional Information: http://www.city.tondabayashi.osaka .jp/foreign/jinaimachi/index.html, http://www5d.biglobe.ne .jp/~heritage

■ Shimo-Akasaka Terraced Rice Fields (下赤阪の棚田)

Rating: 3

A *tanada*, or "terraced rice field," is a type of rice field built on the side of a hill or mountain and formed into steps to make cultivation possible. Japan has long faced the dilemma of a large population living in a small space with very little flat land, and these breathtaking terraced fields can be seen throughout rural parts of the country. The *tanada* of Shimo-Akasaka in Chihaya Village, Osaka Prefecture have been named by the government as one of the top 100 most beautiful terraced rice fields in all of Japan, and photographers swarm in during the autumn season to capture their beautiful colors. Fresh produce is sold on weekends near the bus stop, and at certain times during the autumn season lanterns are set up to illuminate the fields at night.

➢ Access: From Tondabayashi Station (Kintetsu Nagano Line), take a Kongo Bus to Akasaka Chugakko-mae bus stop, and from there walk about 10 min. to the top of the Shimo-Akasaka Castle ruins for a good view of the fields.

➢ Japanese Address: 大阪府南河内郡千早赤阪村大字東阪 25 (middle school located near the fields)

■ Sayama Shrine (狭山神社)

Rating: 1

While it is unclear when the original shrine was built, Sayama Shrine's history is said to go back about 2,000 years. Sayama Shrine is neither large nor awe-inspiring, but it has a simple, humble elegance unique to old, neighborhood shrines. The surrounding neighborhood, composed of traditional wooden houses and small paddy fields, is a joy to walk around. Sayama Shrine's festivals are on July 13 and October 10.

➢ Access: 10 min. on foot from Kongo Station (Nankai Koya Line). Take the west exit from the station, walk until the road begins to curve, and take the first path you see cutting down through the woods. When you come out on a north–south boulevard, turn left and walk until you see the shrine on your left side.

➢ Phone: 072-365-0905

➢ Japanese Address: 大阪府大阪狭山市半田 1-223

Sakai

(Also see the essay on p. 190, "Sakai: Kansai's Lost City")

■ Nanshuji Temple (南宗寺)

Rating: 3

Nanshuji Temple was built in 1557, and after being burned down during the Tokugawa military campaign in Osaka against the Toyotomi and their allies, it was rebuilt in 1617. Although much of Sakai's history was physically lost during Japan's rapid industrialization, Nanshuji stands as a reminder of the city's fascinating and colorful past. Some of the temple's buildings are designated as natural cultural assets, and the Edo Period Zen landscape garden (dry garden) on its grounds is officially designated as a natural scenic spot. There is also a teahouse, which was constructed in 1960 in the style of the famous Sakai tea master Sen no Rikyu.

Even more fascinating is this temple's connections with Sen no Rikyu himself, Sen no Rikyu's teacher, and even Tokugawa Ieyasu, the first shogun from the Tokugawa family (a family that ruled Japan for more than 250 years). One theory about Ieyasu's death suggests that he was assassinated, but the fact was hidden and a counterpart put in his place to prevent the country from falling into turmoil; the grave of the "real" Ieyasu (if this theory is, in fact, true) is hidden away in a corner of Nanshuji Temple.

There is a short but fascinating tour of the temple complex and its buildings and monuments—explanations are in Japanese only, but you can enjoy walking through the complex even if you don't understand the explanations. Visitors can also participate in genuine Zen meditation with the temple's monks every Sunday.

➤ Access: 5–7 min. walk from Goryo-mae Station on the Hankai Streetcar Line. From the platform, turn right at the crosswalk and cross to the sidewalk, turn left and walk straight, take the first right turn, then continue straight until you see the temple entrance on your right side.

➤ Cost: Tours of the complex cost 400 yen for adults, 300 yen for high school and middle school students, and 200 yen for elementary school students.

➤ Open: 9:00 AM to 4:00 PM

➤ Phone: 072-232-1654

➤ Japanese Address: 大阪府堺市堺区南旅篭町東 3-1-2

■ Sakai City Muscum (堺市博物館)

Rating: 3

This history museum tells the fascinating story of Sakai, a unique city that transformed from fishing village to thriving merchant town to industrial megacenter. The Sakai City Museum is compact and focused, with regular exhibits covering the city's history as well special exhibitions on changing themes every spring and autumn. There is even a library of books on Sakai, including some published by the museum itself.

The museum is located near several of the tumuli in the Mozu Tumulus Cluster, including the largest, Nintoku-ryo (see next entry).

- ➤ Access: 6–7 min. walk from Mozu Station on the JR Hanwa Line, or 4 min. walk from Sakai-shi Hakubutsukan-mae bus stop using Nankai Bus #5 from Sakaihigashi Station (Nankai Koya Line). The museum is located in the middle of the relatively large Daisen Park (follow signs for the museum on the park pathways).

- ➤ Cost: 200 yen for adults, 100 yen for university and high school students, and 50 yen for middle and elementary school students (special exhibitions may cost more). Children younger than elementary school age and senior citizens (age 65 or older) may enter for free. Group discounts are available.

- ➤ Open: 9:30 AM to 5:15 PM (last admission at 4:30 PM). Closed on Mondays (or the following day if Monday is a public holiday), the day after each public holiday (unless that day falls on a Saturday or Sunday), and during the New Year's holiday period.

- ➤ Phone: 072-245-6201

- ➤ Japanese Address: 堺市堺区百舌鳥夕雲町 2 丁目(大仙公園)

■ Mozu Tumulus Cluster (百舌鳥古墳群)

Rating: 2

These large tumuli, some of which can be seen from outer space, were built in this ancient imperial center of power starting in the fifth century. The Nintoku-ryo Tumulus (also known as the Daisen Tumulus) is the largest in Japan and the most spectacular, although some of the smaller ones are easier to appreciate from ground level (Nintoku-ryo is so large its shape can only be properly seen from the air). Many tumuli are shaped like keyholes, as Nintoku-ryo is, but they also come in round and square shapes, and they house deceased emperors of ancient Japan. There are more than 48 tumuli in Sakai's Mozu Tumulus cluster, making this the best place in Japan to see these important historical and archeological sites. The Sakai City Museum is located nearby (see previous entry).

➤ Access: Near Mozu Station on the JR Hanwa Line for Nintoku-ryo and surrounding tumuli. You can also use Nankai Bus #5 from Sakaihigashi Station (Nankai Koya Line) and get off at Sakai-shi Hakubutsukan-mae, Daisen-cho, or Mozu-ekimae Bus Stop. Hanzei-ryo is located within walking distance of Sakaihigashi Station (Nankai Koya Line).

➤ Additional Information: http://www.city.sakai.lg.jp/foreigner _en/spot/spot1.html, http://www.city.sakai.lg.jp/city/_rekibun /mozu_en/index.html

➤ Japanese Address: 大阪府堺市堺区大仙町（大仙陵古墳）

■ **Hamadera Park (浜寺公園)**

Rating: 1

Hamadera Park is one of the oldest parks in Osaka, dating back to the nineteenth century. A rose garden with 250 types of roses, lovely pine trees, an outdoor swimming pool with a giant water slide, a miniature train for getting around the park, sports facilities (soccer, archery, baseball, etc.), waterfront walking paths stretching across the spacious park grounds, amusement facilities for children (go-karts, bumper cars, etc.) and more make this a great place to take the family. Furthermore, the cherry blossoms in spring provide a pleasant atmosphere for long walks or relaxing picnics.

Be sure to take a look at the Nankai Hamadera-koen Station building, a beautiful wooden structure built in 1907 and preserved to this day.

➤ Access: Next to Hamaderakoen Station (Nankai main line) and Hamadera-ekimae Station on the Hankai Uemachi Streetcar Line, or a 10 min. walk from Higashi-Hagoromo Station on the JR Hanwa Line.

➤ Open: The train inside the park and the children's facilities are open from 9:00 AM to 5:00 PM and closed on Tuesdays (closed the next day if Tuesday is a public holiday). The pool is open from July 1 to August 31, from 9:30 AM to 6:00 PM (last entry at 5:30 PM). The rose garden is open from March 16 to December 15, from 10:00 AM to 5:00 PM (last entry at 4:30 PM), and it is closed on Tuesdays (closed the next day if Tuesday is a public holiday).

➤ Phone: 072-262-6300

➤ Japanese Address: 大阪府堺市浜寺公園町

■ Myokokuji Temple (妙國寺／妙国寺)

Rating: 1

Myokokuji, one of the head temples of the Nichiren sect of Buddhism, was originally constructed in 1562 and has been destroyed and rebuilt twice since (the current temple is from 1973). The giant cycad tree on the temple grounds is more than 1,100 years old and has been designated as a natural monument; legend has it that Oda Nobunaga, one of the three unifiers of Japan, transplanted the tree in an area that is now part of Shiga Prefecture, but returned it when the tree cried out that it wanted to be returned to Myokokuji Temple.

Myokokuji Temple was made famous by eleven samurai who committed *seppuku*, an incredibly painful form of ritual suicide involving slicing one's own stomach open with a sword (*suppuku* is informally known as *harakiri*, a term more commonly known outside of Japan). This event occurred in response to the Sakai Incident of 1868, a misunderstanding that resulted in the killing of thirteen French sailors: the sailors did not have permission to land at Sakai's port and were killed by Tosa Domain samurai patrolling the city. France demanded compensation, including the deaths of the twenty samurai involved (eleven committed *seppuku* and nine were pardoned and sent back to Tosa). A monument for the eleven who died can be seen at Myokokuji Temple.

➤ Access: 5 min. walk from Myokokuji-mae Station on the Hankai Streetcar Line. Take the small street that goes southeast from the intersection the streetcar stops at (on your left if coming from Osaka City), and continue straight until you see the temple on your right side. It is also a 10–15 min. walk from Sakaihigashi Station on the Nankai Koya Line (check the map at the station for specific directions).

➢ Cost: 400 yen per person

➢ Open: 9:00 AM to 4:00 PM (reservations are required, so please call ahead)

➢ Phone: 072-233-0369

➢ Japanese Address: 大阪府堺市堺区材木町東 4-1-4

■ **Old Sakai Lighthouse (旧堺燈台)**

Rating: 1

Originally built in 1877 (during the Meiji Period), this lighthouse was used to guide ships coming into port until 1968, as Osaka Bay land reclamation projects had rendered it useless by distancing it too much from the sea.

The oldest remaining lighthouse in Japan, the Sakai lighthouse was designed by an English architect and stands at a height of 11.3 meters. It was designated as a national cultural property in 1972. Despite falling into disuse as a navigational beacon, it is still an important piece of history and beloved monument of the citizens of Sakai.

➢ Access: 15 min. walk from Sakai Station on the Nankai main line. From the station, take the west exit and continue going straight until you reach the opposite side of Rihga Royal Hotel Sakai (visible from the station), take a left and continue along that boulevard until you reach the first major intersection, and turn right and go straight along the shore (there were will boats on your right and a park on your left) until you pass underneath the elevated expressway interchange and see the lighthouse.

➢ Japanese Address: 大阪府堺市堺区大浜北町 5-1-22

Fujiidera

■ Domyoji Tenmangu Shrine and Domyoji Temple (道明寺天満宮)

Rating: 2

Domyoji Tenmangu Shrine was founded in 947, and like Tenmangu Shrine in Osaka City (see p. 92), people come here to pray for success in academic endeavors. Domyoji Tenmangu's treasure hall contains six national treasures as well as other priceless relics. The lush shrine complex grounds include approximately 800 plum trees that bloom spectacularly in February and March. Just across the road is Domyoji Temple, which also houses a national treasure: the hand-carved image of the eleven-faced goddess of mercy. The temple was built in the sixth century, during the reign of Emperor Suiko, and it has functioned as an *amadera*, or Buddhist nunnery, since at least the Edo Period (1600–1868).

➢ Access: 3–5 min. walk from Domyoji Station on the Kintetsu Minami-Osaka Line. Walk westward from the station until you come upon the large temple grounds.

➢ Open: The shrine is open from 9:00 AM to 5:00 PM, and the temple from 9:00 AM to 4:00 PM.

➢ Phone: 072-953-2525

➢ Japanese Address: 大阪府藤井寺市道明寺 1-16-40

■ Fujiidera Temple (葛井寺)

Rating: 2

Fujiidera Temple is famous for its stunning wisteria, which bloom in April and May, and also for its thousand-armed *Senju Kannon* statue, a national treasure that is displayed on August 9, the 18th of every month and certain other days. On New Year's Day, many people gather here to ring the temple bell (line up by 1:00 AM if you want to have a chance), pray for the coming year, and drink sake. On other days, the temple is a good place to meet and chat with locals.

The original Fujiidera Temple was built in 725 and many graceful wooden structures and statues grace its grounds. It is located on a long east–west pilgrimage route and has been chosen as one of the best hundred "green" (natural) spots in Osaka Prefecture. Karakuni Shrine is located nearby (see next entry).

➢ Access: 5–7 min. walk from Fujiidera Station on the Kintetsu Minami-Osaka Line. From exit 1 on the station's south side, turn left (while facing the street) and go straight until you come to an intersection with a cross-street that cuts underneath the railroad tracks. Turn right (away from the tracks) and go straight until you see the temple's entry gate on your left side.

➢ Open: 8:00 AM to 5:00 PM

➢ Phone: 072-938-0005

➢ Japanese Address: 大阪府藤井寺市藤井寺 1-16-21

■ Karakuni Shrine (辛國神社)

Rating: 1

This shrine was originally built approximately 1,500 years ago under Emperor Yuryaku, although the current buildings are not nearly that old. Karakuni Shrine is located on a long east–west pilgrimage route that has been chosen as one of the best hundred "green" (natural) spots in Osaka Prefecture. While Karakuni Shrine is not necessarily worth going out of the way to see, you should stop by if visiting the nearby Fujiidera Temple (see previous entry). I originally discovered Karakuni Shrine when I took a wrong turn on my way to Fujiidera Temple, but I was pleasantly surprised by the little shrine's unique charm.

➢ Access: 5–7 min. walk from Fujiidera Station on the Kintetsu Minami-Osaka Line. From exit 1 on the station's south side, turn left (while facing the street) and go straight until you come to an intersection with a cross-street that cuts underneath the railroad tracks. Turn right (away from the tracks) and go straight, past the entrance to Fujiidera Temple (see previous entry), continuing until you see the shrine's entrance on your right side.

- ➢ Open: Facilities are open from 9:00 AM to 4:00 PM, but the temple gates are open from 6:00 AM to 5:00 PM.
- ➢ Phone: 072-955-2473
- ➢ Japanese Address: 大阪府藤井寺市藤井寺 1-19-14

Kishiwada/Izumisano/KIX

■ Kishiwada Castle (岸和田城)

Rating: 3

It is believed that Kishiwada Castle, also known as Chikiri Castle, was originally built in 1334. It changed ownership many times as retainers of Oda Nobunaga, Toyotomi Hideyoshi, and the Tokugawa family resided here, and it played an important role as the center of rule in the Kishiwada Domain (until the late nineteenth century) and as a southern defense for Osaka. The keep was destroyed when it was struck by lightning in 1827, and it was rebuilt in its current form in 1954 (there were numerous rebuildings previous to this, and the five-storey keep was reduced to three storeys from 1585 rebuildings onward). The castle grounds contain the lovely Hachi-no-Niwa rock garden (best when viewed from above, from the castle keep), and the castle itself has exhibits of various artifacts inside.

There is a natural history museum nearby, a shrine (Kishiki Shrine) that plays an important part in the Danjiri Matsuri festival held every autumn (see p. 178), and an upscale restaurant with a lovely old Japanese garden (Gofuso) on the castle's southwest side that can be viewed for free.

- ➢ Access: 10 min. walk west from Kishiwada Station or 7 min. walk north from Takojizo Station (both on the Nankai main line). Takojizo Station is most convenient for visiting Kishiwada Castle and the Kishiwada Danjiri Hall (see next entry), but you have to switch from an express to a local train at Kishiwada Station to get there. If walking from Kishiwada Station, continue southwest along the boulevard running past the north side of the station until you reach the first major intersection (the first traffic signal), continue straight across the street onto a smaller street and keep going until that street curves right, then continue straight after that right turn until you see the castle on your right side (after passing a school). If walking from Takojizo Station, take exit 1 (north side of the station) and turn right when you exit to the street, and continue straight along that small street (which will curve to the right soon) until you reach a T-intersection, at which point you need to turn left and go straight until you see the castle.

- ➢ Cost: Entrance to view exhibitions and go to the top of the castle keep is 300 yen for adults and free for middle school students and younger. A combination ticket is available for 700 yen that admits you to Kishiwada Castle, Kishiwada Danjiri Hall (see next entry) and the Natural History Museum (not included in this guidebook).

- ➢ Open: 10:00 AM to 5:00 PM (last admission at 4:00 PM). Closed on Mondays (except public holidays) and during the New Year's holiday period.

- ➢ Phone: 072-431-3251

- ➢ Additional Information: http://www.jcastle.info/castle/profile /67-Kishiwada-Castle (information on the Jcastle website)

- ➢ Japanese Address: 大阪府岸和田市岸城町 9-1

■ Kishiwada Danjiri Hall (岸和田だんじり会館)

Rating: 3

The Kishiwada Matsuri festival (held in autumn—see p. 178) is one of the most dangerous festivals in Japan, with people injured (and sometimes worse) every year, but it is an important part of local history and culture for residents of Kishiwada. Regardless of whether or not you see the festival in person, the Kishiwada Danjiri Hall is a great place to learn about the local customs of Kishiwada and Osaka Prefecture. The facility exhibits Danjiri floats, which are raced at blistering speeds through the streets by swarms of youths as people dance on top. There are also historical records, displays of intricate woodcarving done for the floats, clothing and lanterns used at the festival, and more on display. Two video presentations—one a three-screen wide-view introduction to the festival, and one a 3D video enabling visitors to experience riding through the crowds on a float—help you get a feel for what it's like to actually see the exciting festival in person.

➤ Access: 13 min. walk west from Kishiwada Station or 10 min. walk north from Takojizo Station (both on the Nankai main line). Takojizo Station is best for seeing this facility and Kishiwada Castle (see previous entry), but you have to switch from an express to a local train at Kishiwada Station to get there. The hall is located behind Kishiwada Castle (see directions in previous entry for Kishiwada Castle).

➤ Cost: Admission is 600 yen for adults and 300 for children. A combination ticket is available for 700 yen that admits you to the Kishiwada Danjiri Hall, Kishiwada Castle (see previous entry) and the Natural History Museum (not included in this guidebook). Group discounts are also available.

➤ Open: 10:00 AM to 5:00 PM (last admission at 4:00 PM). Closed on Mondays (except Mondays following public holidays), and from December 30 to January 4.

➤ Phone: 072-431-1010

➤ Japanese Address: 大阪府岸和田市本町 11-23

■ Rinku Town (りんくうタウン)

Rating: 3

Conveniently located near Kansai International Airport (see next entry) and stations on two major rail lines (JR and Nankai), Rinku Town is one of the best shopping areas in Osaka Prefecture. Rinku Premium Outlets is an outlet store complex with great deals on international brands, and best of all (for expats living in Kansai) it has imported clothes in their original sizes. The shopping center is located near the sea, and there is a rocky beach (Marble Beach) from which you can see planes taking off and landing at the island airport. The Rinku Pleasure Town Seacle shopping center is also nearby, and its main attraction is the giant Ferris wheel offering sweeping views of the entire bay area. Rinku Town is also home to the Rinku Gate

Tower Building, which is tied as the second-highest building in Japan with Osaka City's Cosmo Tower (see p. 120). Rinku Gate Tower houses the ANA Gate Tower Hotel and is connected directly to Rinku-town Station.

➢ Access: Shopping and entertainment facilities are located within a 5–10 min. walk of Rinku-town Station (Nankai main line/ Airport Line and JR Hanwa Line trains bound for the airport).

➢ Cost: The giant Ferris wheel at Rinku Pleasure Town Seacle costs 700 yen per person.

➢ Open: Rinku Premium Outlets is open from 10:00 AM to 8:00 PM every day (but closed on the third Thursday of February). Rinku Pleasure Town Seacle is open from 10:00 AM to 8:00 PM, and the Ferris wheel is open from 10:00 AM to 9:00 PM.

➢ Phone: 072-458-4600 (Rinku Premium Outlets), 072-461-4196 (Rinku Pleasure Town Seacle)

➢ Additional Information: http://www.premiumoutlets.co.jp/en /rinku (Rinku Premium Outlets)

➢ Japanese Address: 大阪府泉佐野市りんくう往来南 3-28 (Rinku Premium Outlets), 大阪府泉佐野市りんくう往来南 3番地 (Rinku Pleasure Town Seacle)

■ **Kansai International Airport (関西国際空港)**

Rating: 1

Kansai International Airport (KIX) is one of the busiest air transport hubs in Japan and the main airport for the Kansai region. It is located on an artificial island in Osaka Bay, and the completion of the island bumped Osaka up from smallest prefecture in Japan (in terms of land area) to second-smallest, overtaking Kagawa Prefecture in Shikoku. The airport is connected to the mainland by a 3-kilometer (1.9-mile) bridge that carries rail and road traffic, and also by ferry services. The terminal building was designed by world-famous Italian architect Renzo Piano, and because it is the world's longest terminal at 1.7 kilometers (1.1 miles) in length it is served by its own tram line. There are two runways, and a third is planned as part of a future expansion. KIX has a good variety of restaurants and facilities, and just across the bridge is Rinku Town (see previous entry), one of the best shopping districts in prefectural Osaka.

➢ Access: Get off at Kansai-Airport Station. Nankai lines bound for the airport start at Namba, and JR lines bound for the airport start at Kyobashi or Osaka (with the exception of the limited express, which starts in Kyoto) and follow the Osaka Loop Line counterclockwise until Tennoji before splitting off onto the Hanwa Line.

➢ Additional Information: http://www.kansai-airport.or.jp/en /index.asp

Northern Osaka Prefecture Sightseeing Guide

Overview

Northern Osaka Prefecture is filled with quiet bedroom towns, but amongst these sleepy neighborhoods await some of the most impressive cultural sights Osaka has to offer. Delightfully tranquil temples, the legendary Banpaku Memorial Park, an unparalleled open-air museum featuring ancient architecture, the most beautiful stretch of nature in the prefecture can be discovered here.

Toyonaka/Ikeda/Minoh

■ Minoh Park (箕面公園)

Rating: 5

Minoh Park (formally known as Meiji-no-Mori Minoh Quasi-National Park) is one of the most gorgeous natural spots in the entire Kansai region. Amid lush forests and rocky slopes is Minoh Waterfall, the park's centerpiece at a height of 33 meters (108 feet). The Tokai Nature trail starts from Minoh Park, and the area is filled with low-lying peaks ranging from 100 to 600 meters (approx. 330 to 1,970 feet) in height. Over 1,000 plants species and 3,000 insect species, as well as a large number of animal species, can be observed here, and there is even an insect museum. Adorable (but mischievous) monkeys walk the trails and roads, striking photogenic poses and occasionally snatching food from the hands of inattentive tourists.

      Ryuanji, a beautiful old temple in the park that is popular among visitors and locals alike, gives testament to the area's historical importance as a Buddhist spiritual center. The tomb of

Kaijyo, an important Buddhist monk who founded the temple of Katsuoji in 765 in Minoh City, is also located in Minoh Park.

One of the most enjoyable aspects of Minoh Park is seeing it throughout the changing seasons: the fiery colors of autumn, snowy slopes and branches heavy with icicles in winter, vibrant pinks and whites of spring cherry blossoms, and lush greens of the forest set against the bright blue skies of summer are all equally brilliant to behold.

➢ Access: Take the Hankyu Takarazuka Line from Umeda Station, transfer to the Mino-o Line at Ishibashi Station, and get off at Mino-o Station (the terminus). It is a 10–15 min. walk north from the station. You can also go to Senri-chuo Station on the Midosuji Subway Line / Kita-Osaka Kyuko Line and take a Hankyu Bus bound for "Mino-o eki" to get to Mino-o Station.

➢ Phone: 072-721-3014

➢ Note: Please do not litter or do anything that may damage the natural environment or disturb animals or their habitats while visiting the park. Do not feed the monkeys. As a visitor to this park, it is your duty to help preserve its natural beauty.

➢ Japanese Address: 大阪府箕面市箕面公園 1-18

■ Open-Air Museum of Old Japanese Farmhouses (日本民家集落博物館)

Rating: 3

If you are at all interested in traditional architecture, this outdoor museum is a destination you can't afford to miss. In order to preserve Japan's traditional houses, such structures have been relocated here from all corners of Japan, giving visitors a rare opportunity to view traditional Japanese buildings complete with earthen floors and thatched roofs. The houses can be explored inside and out, and you can drink tea while sitting around an old-fashioned *irori* hearth inside one of the houses. There's even a *kabuki* stage! For those interested in architecture, this open-air museums contains some rare gems that are vanishing from even the farthest reaches of the Japanese countryside.

- ➢ Access: 15 min. walk from Ryokuchi-koen Station (Kita-Osaka Kyuko Line, which has through services from the Midosuji Subway Line). Walk west from the station until you enter the large park, and then follow park signs and maps to reach the museum.

- ➢ Cost: 500 for adults, 300 for high school students, 200 for middle and elementary school students, and free for children younger than that. Group discounts are available.

- ➢ Open: 9:30 AM to 5:00 PM (last admission at 4:30 PM). Closed on Mondays (the following day if Monday is a public holiday), and from December 27 to January 4.

- ➢ Phone: 06-6862-3137

- ➢ Japanese Address: 大阪府豊中市服部緑地 1-2

■ Daikoji Temple (大広寺)

Rating: 2

This temple complex, which belongs to the Soto sect of Buddhism, was founded in 1395. It stretches up a mountainside in the semi-rural suburb of Ikeda City. A climb up the mossy stone steps takes you to the center of the complex, where you will come face to face with a gorgeous temple gate and sweeping view of the surrounding Ikeda City, as well as nearby Toyonaka and Kawanishi Cities. Some parts of this little-known temple have even survived intact since the seventeenth century. In particular, be sure to take time to appreciate the truly impressive, intricate wood carvings on the gate at the top.

- ➢ Access: From Ikeda Station (Hankyu Takarazuka Line), ride Hankyu Bus #1 or #11 to Satsukiyama-koen Daikoji bus stop (approx. 15 min. ride). Climb the small staircase behind the bus stop, then climb the large staircase after that up toward the temple. Be careful when the staircase is wet during or after rain, as it becomes incredibly slippery.

- ➢ Phone: 072-751-3433

- ➢ Japanese Address: 大阪府池田市綾羽 2-5-16

■ Hagi-no-tera Toko-in Temple (萩の寺 東光院)

Rating: 1

This Sento sect Buddhist temple traces its roots back to 735 when it was founded by Gyoki, a Buddhist priest who also played an important part in the construction of Todaiji Temple in Nara. The temple was moved to its current location in 1914 when Hankyu Railways built its Takarazuka Line. Toko-in's common name, Hagi-no-tera, refers to the many *hagi* (bush clovers) on the temple grounds (Hagi-no-tera means "temple of bush clovers"). Although this temple was famous in ancient times, it eventually fell into obscurity and disrepair, but recent renovations and rebuilding projects have somewhat restored it to its former glory. Today, Toko-in is in possession of several valuable drawings and Buddhist images. Its narrow paths, lush vegetation, beautiful old buildings and carvings, and jungle-like grounds punctuated only by the sounds of birds and insects make this quiet neighborhood temple a pleasure to visit.

➤ Access: 5 min. walk from Sone Station on the Hankyu Takarazuka Line (ride the local if you are coming from Hanyku Umeda Station).

➤ Open: 9:00 AM to 5:00 PM

➤ Phone: 06-6852-3002

➤ Additional Information: http://en.wikipedia.org/wiki/Gyoki (short biography of Gyoki)

➤ Japanese Address: 大阪府豊中市南桜塚 1-12-7

Suita/Ibaraki

■ Banpaku Memorial Park (万博記念公園)

Rating: 4

The Expo '70 Commemorative Park, more commonly called Banpaku Koen in Japanese (referred to as Banpaku Memorial Park in the guidebook), was the site of the World's Fair of 1970, a symbolic event that spurred rapid growth in Osaka much like the

1964 Olympic Games did in Tokyo. It was also an event that exhibited Japan's postwar progress for the world to see. The park itself was planned by famed architect Kenzo Tange, and the Tower of the Sun (*Taiyo no To*), designed by celebrated modern artist Taro Okamoto, is the symbol of this park and an Osaka landmark that has become famous throughout the country. Although this peculiar tower was initially criticized by many, it is now a beloved piece of art among Kansai locals.

The expansive, 98-hectare park grounds are home to the National Museum of Ethnology (see next entry) and Expo '70 Commemorative Stadium (see p. 153), which I have handled in separate sections. In addition, there is a massive Japanese garden complete with tea houses—a tranquil place where you can easily pass the entire day roaming the many walking paths. There are also a number of event facilities, refreshing trails amidst the park's greenery, the Japan Folk Crafts Museum, and even a time capsule set up by Matsushita (Panasonic) and Mainichi Newspapers scheduled to be open in the year 6970 (5,000 years after Expo '70). The National Museum of Art (see p. 83) was originally located here, but has since been moved to a new facility on Nakanoshima in central Osaka City.

➤ Access: The park is directly outside of Bampaku-kinen-koen Station on the Osaka Monorail main line. It can also be accessed from Koen-higashiguchi Station on the Osaka Monorail Saito Line (this station is closest to the Japanese garden). From central Osaka, the easiest way to reach the Osaka Monorail is to take the Midosuji Line / Kita-Osaka Kyuko Line to Senri-chuo Station and transfer there. Park maps are available at the entrance.

➤ Costs and Hours: Park entrance alone costs 250 yen for adults and 70 yen for children (middle school students or younger). Facilities inside have separate fees, but combination tickets (including park entrance) are available. Most facilities are open from 9:30 AM to 5:00 PM and are closed during the New Year's holiday period, but hours and holidays vary by facility. Refer to the website (see below) for detailed information.

➤ Phone: 06-6687-7387

➢ Additional Information: http://www.expo70.or.jp/e/index.html

➢ Japanese Address: 大阪吹田市千里万博公園 1-1

■ National Museum of Ethnology (国立民族学博物館)

Rating: 3

Located inside Banpaku Memorial Park (see previous entry) and first opened in 1977, this outstanding museum has 255,000 artifacts, 12,000 of which are displayed at a time. It is also an important research center, with 60 academic researchers working actively in ethnology and related fields as well as graduate studies programs. The museum aims to provide visitors with accurate and current information on societies all around the world.

Where the museum really shines is the quality of its exhibits. There are a number of simulated environments and interactive segments, so you will not find yourself merely looking at glass displays of pots and hunting tools accompanied by dry explanations. Furthermore, the content covers social groups from all corners of the earth, past and present, and does so in a truly interesting manner that will leave you wanting to learn more after you leave. Audio guides in multiple languages can be rented to enhance your museum-browsing experience, and the overall progression and layouts of exhibits are smooth and well organized. Special exhibitions are sometimes held, displaying rare ethnological materials borrowed from other institutions.

➢ Access: Located inside Banpaku Memorial Park, a 15 min. walk from Banpaku-kinen-koen Station (Osaka Monorail main line) and Koen-higashiguchi Station (Osaka Monorail Saito Line). Park maps that show the museum's location are available at the entrance.

➢ Cost: 420 for adults, 250 for college and high school students, 110 yen for middle and elementary school students. Combi-nation tickets including admission to the museum are available at the Banpaku Memorial Park entrance gates. Group discounts are available.

- Open: 10:00 AM to 5:00 PM (last admission at 4:30 PM). Closed on Wednesdays (closed the next day if Wednesday is a public holiday) and from December 28 to January 4.
- Phone: 06-6876-2151
- Additional Information: http://www.minpaku.ac.jp/english
- Japanese Address: 大阪府吹田市千里万博公園 10-1

■ Expo '70 Commemorative Stadium (Gamba Osaka Soccer Stadium) (万博記念競技場)

Rating: 2

Expo '70 Commemorative Stadium is the home stadium of Suita City–based soccer team Gamba Osaka, one of the top teams in the J-League since their debut in 1993. The word "Gamba" comes from the Italian word for leg, and also the Japanese word *ganbaru* which means "give it your all!" The team's most vocal supporters sit in the northern part of the stadium, so if you want to join in and cheer Gamba on, that's place to sit. Fans of live soccer in Japan need look no further than this stadium and this team.

- Access: 2 min. walk from Koen-hagashiguchi Station (Osaka Monorail Saito Line), next to the east entrance for Banpaku Memorial Park (see p. 150).
- Phone: 06-6875-8111
- Additional Information: http://www.gamba-osaka.net/en/index .html (Gamba Osaka's official website, featuring team, ticket and schedule information)
- Japanese Address: 大阪府吹田市千里万博公園 5-2 （万博記念競技場）

■ Sojiji Temple (総持寺)

Rating: 2

Sojiji Temple is number 22 on the famous 33-temple Saigoku pilgrimage route, and it has been a popular destination for worshippers and travelers alike since the Heian Period (approximately 1,000 years ago). The *kannon* enshrined here is said to help in child-raising and ward off evil. When the Saigoku pilgrimage route began to gain popularity at a rapid pace (several hundred years ago), most people were traveling around the Kansai region on foot, meaning a large amount of time was needed to complete the pilgrimage; this temple was included in a "mini-pilgrimage" for people who could not take months out of their life and make the entire 33-temple trek. Even today, with modern private and public transportation, visiting all the temples is quite a feat. Sojiji Temple is not only a lovely temple on its own, its easy access by rail provides a great chance to sample part of the pilgrim's journey.

➤ Access: 5–7 min. walk from Sojiji Station on the Hankyu Kyoto Line (express trains don't stop here, so it's quickest to take an express train to Ibaraki or Takatsuki Station and then switch to a local train for Sojiji Station). From the west-side exit of the station, take the middlemost of the three streets going away from the train tracks at the first small intersection you see (the small street on the left side of the pachinko & slot parlor), follow that until you reach a T-intersection, then turn left and go straight until you see the temple on your right.

➤ Open: The gates are open from 6:00 AM to 5:00 PM.

➤ Phone: 072-622-3209

➤ Japanese Address: 大阪府茨木市総持寺 1-6-1

Eastern Osaka Prefecture Sightseeing Guide

Overview

Eastern Osaka Prefecture is a diverse mix of nature, down-to-earth suburban culture, and unique sightseeing spots. Mount Ikoma, which straddles the border separating Osaka and Nara Prefectures, offers a sweeping view of the Osaka metropolitan area. It is also home to Hozanji Temple, one of the most stunning (and relatively undiscovered) temples in the entire Kansai region. Ishikiri-Tsurugiya Shrine, hidden away in Higashiosaka and surrounded by tea and fortune teller shops, is just one place where you can experience the same traditions and lifestyles that locals do. And Hiraoka Shrine provides a tranquil, wooded sanctuary atop a ridge overlooking a vast suburban landscape.

Moriguchi/Higashiosaka

■ Ishikiri-Tsurugiya Shrine (石切劔箭神社)

Rating: 3

Ishikiri-Tsurugiya Shrine, located in Higashiosaka City, is popular among local residents. The tradition at this temple is to walk around two stones placed in front of the temple one hundred times while praying in order to help loved ones who are sick or suffering. On weekends, large crowds can be seen walking in circles in front of the temple's main hall. In addition, the shop-lined street leading from Ishikiri Station is popular for its many fortune-telling shops, and the area surrounding the temple has numerous small shops selling local tea. To get off the beaten track and experience local traditions and a quieter side of Japanese life, this is a good place to start.

➤ Access: 10–15 min. walk from Ishikiri Station (Kintetsu Nara Line), or 5–7 min. from Shin-Ishikiri Station (Kintetsu Keihanna Line). From exit 2 on the west side of Ishikiri Station, turn left and walk south along the small street until you can't go straight anymore, then turn right and follow that road until you reach the shrine (there are shrine-like gates along the way). From Shin-Ishikiri Station, take exit 4, and after descending to ground level (you will be at an intersection with a traffic signal), walk straight ahead in the direction you are facing and turn left at the first small street you see, walk straight from there and turn right at the second small street, then continue straight until you see the shrine on your left.

➤ Phone: 072-982-3621

➤ Japanese Address: 大阪府東大阪市東石切町 1-1-1

■ Hiraoka Shrine (枚岡神社)

Rating: 2

This shrine's long history predates the first emperor of Japan (Emperor Jimmu). Located in the former province of Kawachi and hidden away on a wooded slope, this shrine has been an important part of the local area since ancient times, and the current central shrine building was completed in 1826. In winter, the *ume* plum trees blossom to create a spectacular scene, and the view overlooking the Osaka suburbs from the temple's sleepy mountain town can be enjoyed year-round. Be sure to take time to admire the beautiful wooden *torii* gate at the entrance.

Situated only about 25–30 minutes from Namba, this quiet shrine makes for a refreshing getaway from the city's hustle and bustle.

➤ Access: 2 min. walk from Hiraoka Station on the Kintetsu Nara Line (only local trains and suburban semi-express trains stop here, with the latter being fastest). When you exit the station (when coming from Namba), cross the tracks and head uphill until you reach the shrine.

➤ Phone: 072-981-4177

➤ Japanese Address: 大阪府東大阪市出雲井町 7-16

Mount Ikoma

■ Hozanji Temple (宝山寺)

Rating: 5

Hozanji Temple provides a good example of something I believe strongly about travel in Japan: sometimes the best places to visit are also places that few people know about. This old temple on Mount Ikoma, beloved by locals but almost unknown outside of the Kansai region, has an elegance, dignity, and awe-inspiring sense of presence you will encounter at few other places. Although Hozanji Temple is technically in Nara Prefecture (Mount Ikoma is right on the prefectural border), culturally and geographically it is more strongly connected to Osaka, and it was around long before modern prefectures existed, so I have included it in this guidebook.

Hozanji is a mountain temple that truly feels like a mountain temple. Rather than the bright vermilion color typical of Buddhist architectural design, Hozanji displays a rich mix of natural wooden hues, which bring out the age of its stately buildings and help it melt seamlessly into the forested mountain scenery. The thatched roofs are beautiful, resembling those of ancient Shinto shrines more than those of a typical Buddhist temple.

It is an ancient and relatively secluded temple with a history dating back to the beginnings of Japanese civilization, and it was often used as a training ground for Buddhist monks. The current Hozanji was reopened in the seventeenth century, at which time its popularity grew significantly as recreational travel became increasingly popular Japan.

This temple is one of the greatest hidden treasures not just in Osaka, but in the Kansai region. I highly recommend making it a top priority in your travel itinerary.

➢ Access: 10 min. walk from Hozanji Station on the Ikoma Cable Line (transfer to this cable car line at Kintetsu Ikoma Station on the Kintetsu Nara Line, Kintetsu Ikoma Line and Kintetsu Keihanna Line). Be forewarned that the walk from Hozanji Station involves a moderate amount of stair-climbing. When you leave Hozanji Station, you will be on a small, curving path:

follow this until you come to a four-way intersection, at which point you need to take the staircase directly across from you (do not take the paths to your left or right). This staircase will curve around and bring you directly to Hozanji Temple.

➢ Open: 8:00 AM to 4:00 PM

➢ Phone: 0743-73-2006

➢ Japanese Address: 奈良県生駒市門前町 1-1

■ Mount Ikoma Summit (生駒山山頂)

Rating: 3

Although the main destination to see on Mount Ikoma is nearby Hozanji Temple (see previous entry), the summit provides a good, unobstructed view of Osaka City and many of its surrounding suburbs. The sea of lights that can be seen at night from the summit is especially impressive. Additionally, Kintetsu runs cable cars to the top of the mountain, making access convenient.

There is a small amusement park called Skyland Ikoma on top (great for kids), some nice areas to walk around and take in the natural scenery, and even some longer hiking trails going down the mountain (recommended if you have the time).

➢ Access: Near Ikoma Sanjo Station on the Ikoma Cable Line (transfer to this cable car line at Kintetsu Ikoma Station on the Kintetsu Nara Line, Kintetsu Ikoma Line and Kintetsu Keihanna Line). The best view from the summit can be had by walking to the back side of Skyland Ikoma.

➢ Cost: Entry to Skyland Ikoma is free, but attractions are not (most cost 300 yen per ride).

➢ Open: Skyland Ikoma is generally open from 10:00 AM to 5:00 PM, but hours vary by season.

➢ Phone: 0743-74-2173 (Skyland Ikoma)

➢ Additional Information: http://ww4.tiki.ne.jp/~mmurakami /setoy/kinki/e_narukawa.html (panoramic view from the summit of Mount Ikoma)

➢ Japanese Address: 大阪府東大阪市山手町 2017-3 (Ikoma Skyland)

Okonomiyaki Guide

What is Okonomiyaki?

One of Osaka's most well-known foods is *okonomiyaki*, which can be literally translated as "cook what you like." Shaped liked a large pancake or small pizza (but thicker), okonomiyaki contains eggs, *dashi* cooking stock, cabbage and other vegetables, and usually pork or seafood of some sort. It is topped with mayonnaise, sauce, *aonori* (dried seaweed flakes), *katsuo dashi* (bonito flakes), and sometimes cheese. Okonomiyaki sometimes contains other ingredients such as *kimchi*, bacon and green onions. The dish described above is known as Kansai-style or Osaka-style okonomiyaki. Two other places that are known for their variations of okonomiyaki are Hiroshima and Tokyo. Hiroshima's is made a bit differently, using layers of ingredients and noodles rather than a solid, fluffy okonomiyaki as in Osaka. Tokyo's *monjayaki* is a goopy mess that isn't worth your time. Debates can become intense when comparing the merits of Osaka- and Hiroshima-style okonomiyaki, because both are delicious and loved in their respective regions.

Osaka has a nearly endless selection of okonomiyaki shops. The following list contains recommendations of personal favorites as well as famous shops you may want to check out to get started. I have personally eaten at each restaurant below. Shops are listed in romanized alphabetical order.

Okonomiyaki Restaurants

■ Bonhan (ぼん繁)

This is a shop I came across by chance while living in Tenmabashi, and it has been one of my favorites ever since. The prices are more than fair, and you get a lot of food for what you pay. Each and every okonomiyaki is fluffy and savory, and you can customize it by choosing from a wide range of ingredients. *Buta-tama* (pork) with cheese is particularly tasty here.

➢ Access: 1–2 min. on foot from Temmabashi Station (Tanimachi Subway Line, Keihan lines). From the subway station, take exit 1 and cross the street (across from the OMM building, near a bus stop). From the Keihan station, go out the east exit and cross the street diagonally (when the traffic signal changes at this intersection, pedestrians cross in all directions at once).

➢ Hours: 11:30 AM to 10:40 PM (last order at 10:00 PM), but until 9:40 PM (last order at 9:00 PM) on Saturdays. Closed on Sundays and public holidays.

➢ Phone: 06-6943-9361

➢ Japanese Address: 大阪市中央区大手前 1-6-7

■ Boteju (ぼてぢゅう)

Boteju is one of the "big three" okonomiyaki shops in Osaka (the others being Fugetsu and Chibo), and it's a safe bet if you want to try quality food at one of Osaka's most famous restaurants. Aside from shops all around the Kansai region, Boteju has branches in prefectures as far away as Okayama, Aichi, Kanagawa, Tokyo and Yamanashi.

➢ Access: The easiest branch to find in Minami is the Dotombori shop (the head shop in Osaka), which is near the south side of Ebisubashi Bridge (see p. 49) and the south entrance to the Shinsaibashi Shopping Arcade (see p. 68), just a few minutes away from Namba Station on the Midosuji, Sennichimae and Yotsubashi Subway Lines, as well as Osaka-Namba Station on the Kintetsu lines and Hanshin Namba Line. In Kita (Umeda), there is a shop on the 7th floor of the HEP NAVIO building (see p. 75), located near Umeda Station on the Midosuji Subway Line, Hankyu lines, and Hanshin Main Line; Higashi Umeda Station on the Tanimachi Subway Line; and JR Osaka Station.

➢ Hours: The Dotombori shop is open from 11:00 AM to midnight (last order at 11:00 PM) on weekdays, and 10:00 AM to 11:00 PM (last order at 10:30 PM) on weekends and public holidays. The HEP NAVIO branch in Umeda is open from 11:00 AM to 10:30 PM (last order at 9:30 PM) every day.

➢ Phone: 050-5816-4807 (Dotombori shop), 06-6316-1455 (HEP NAVIO branch)

➢ Additional Information: http://www.botejyu.com/group

➢ Japanese Address: 大阪市中央区道頓堀 1-6-15 Comrade ドウトンビル 2F (Dotombori shop), 大阪市北区角田町 7-10 HEP ナビオ 7F (HEP NAVIO branch)

■ **Chibo (千房)**

Chibo is one of the "big three" ramen shops in Osaka (the others being Boteju and Fugetsu), and one that places great emphasis on quality—a quality that encompasses not only the okonomiyaki itself, but the toppings (*aonori*, sauce, etc.) placed on the finished food. Although the prices may be a bit steeper than at other shops, there are many unique menu items and a good-tasting meal is guaranteed.

➢ Access: The Sennichimae main shop is a 5 min. walk from exit 5 of Namba Station on the Midosuji and Sennichimae Subway Lines from Nankai Namba Station. Walk to the first street to the north of the old Namba Grand Kagetsu Theatre building (see directions on p. 65) and turn right; you will see the shop on the left side of the street. There are other shops in Dotombori and Shinsaibashi. There is also a branch in Umeda inside Herbis Plaza Umeda, a 5 min. walk from the Kitashinchi Station on the JR Tozai Line and Nishi-Umeda Station on the Yotsubashi Subway Line, and a 10 min. walk from JR Osaka Station and Umeda Station on the Midosuji Subway Line and Hanshin Main Line.

➢ Hours: Vary by shop, but most are open from 11:00 AM until early morning the next day (except for the Umeda branch, which closes at 11:00 PM). Last order is generally an hour before closing.

- ➢ Phone: 06-6643-0111 (Sennichimae shop), 06-6343-7113 (Umeda branch)

- ➢ Japanese Address: 大阪市中央区難波千日前 11-27 道風ビル 1F〜2F (Sennichimae shop), 大阪市北区梅田 2-5-25 バービス PLAZA B2 (Umeda branch)

■ Fugetsu (鶴橋風月)

With its main shop in Tsuruhashi (see p. 105), Fugetsu is the third of the "big three" ramen shops in Osaka (the others being Boteju and Chibo), and it's one of the most widely known Osakan restaurants in Japan, with branches as far away as Saitama and Fukuoka. Fugetsu's flavor does, of course, suffer a bit because it has become a huge chain, but it still offers quality food and the chance to eat at the most famous of all okonomiyaki restaurants. Bottom line: you won't be disappointed with Fugetsu.

- ➢ Access: The head shop is in Tsuruhashi, just steps away from Tsuruhasi Station on the Sennichimae Line (exit 7), Kintetsu lines, and the JR Osaka Loop Line. The easiest branch to find by far is the one in Namba, which is located in the Namba Grand Building directly outside of exit 24 of Namba Station on the Midosuji, Sennichimae and Yotsubashi Subway Lines (also near Osaka-Namba Station on the Hanshin Namba Line and Kintetsu lines)—the shop is located on the building's B1 floor. Finally, the Umeda shop is located near Higashi-Umeda Station on the Tanimachi Subway Line, and also relatively close to Umeda Station on the Midosuji Subway Line, Umeda Station on the Hankyu lines and Hanshin Main Line, and JR Osaka Station—from the Hankyu-mae (阪急前) intersection, go east on the large boulevard until you see Fugetsu on your right side.

- ➢ Hours: Vary by shop, but most are open from 11:00 AM to 11:00 PM, with last order an hour before closing. The Umeda shop is open until 11:15 PM on weekdays, public holidays and Sundays, and until 3:00 AM on Saturdays and days preceding public holidays.

- Phone: 06-6771-7938 (Tsuruhashi shop), 06-6214-5215 (Namba Grand Bldg. branch), 06-6314-2233 (Umeda branch)

- Additional Information: http://www.ideaosaka.co.jp/web /english/index.html

- Japanese Address: 大阪市天王寺区下味原町 2-18 (Tsuruhashi shop), 大阪市中央区難波 2-2-3 御堂筋グランドビル B1 (Namba Grand Bldg. branch), 大阪市北区曾根崎 2-16-22 アメリカンビル B1〜2F (Umeda Branch)

■ Fukuya (ふくや)

You will have to take a short train ride to Juso (see p. 77) to eat at Fukuya, but it is well worth the trip. This friendly neighborhood shop is frequented mostly by locals, resulting in an atmosphere entirely different from that of popular chain shops in more central parts of town. Fukuya offers a variety of different dishes at reasonable prices, but their home-style okonomiyaki is the first thing you should try—each okonomiyaki is carefully cooked to perfection using only the freshest ingredients.

- Access: Take the west exit from Juso Station (Hankyu Kobe, Takarazuka and Kyoto Lines). After exiting the station, walk straight until you reach a large three-way intersection, then go straight across the street and enter the covered shopping arcade directly in front of you (there should be a McDonald's on your right just as you enter the shopping arcade). Walk straight and take the third right turn (near a Lawson convenience store), then continue walking until you see Fukuya on your left (if you come out onto a boulevard, you've gone too far).

- Hours: 7:00 PM to 4:00 AM. Closed on Sundays.

- Phone: 06-6303-9187

- Japanese Address: 大阪市淀川区十三本町 1-21-31

■ Okaru (おかる)

With a history of more than six decades and a location right in the heart of Minami, Okaru knows how to do okonomiyaki right. The cooks employ a secret cooking method and top-notch ingredients to bring out the rich flavor of every element of the dish. After the okonomiyaki is finished, the staff will draw face, a popular cartoon character, or even a famous Osaka landmark on top of your okonomiyaki with the mayonnaise topping.

> Access: Okaru is nearly equidistant from Nippombashi Station (Sakaisuji and Sennichimae Subway Lines, Kintetsu lines) and Namba Station (Midosuji, Sennichimae and Yotsubashi Subway Lines; Kintetsu lines; Hanshin Namba Line). Walk east from exit 15-A of Namba Station or west from exit 2 of Nippombashi Station (you should be walking along a boulevard underneath an expressway) until you see the entrance to the Sennichimae Shopping Arcade across the street (next to Bic Camera). From there, turn north and walk straight, take the next right turn down a tiny street, and you will see Okaru on your right side.

> Hours: Noon to 3:00 PM, 5:00 PM to 10:30 PM. Closed on Thursdays.

> Phone: 06-6211-0985

> Japanese Address: 大阪市中央区千日前 1-9-19

■ **Takohachi (たこはち)**

This little shop may not look like much at first glance, but it only takes one bite to understand why I included it in this list. Located in the middle of Tsuruhashi (see p. 105), Takohachi is surrounded by a large number of popular Korean-style *yakiniku* restaurants, but it has made a name for itself despite the steep competition. Its sweet, fluffy okonomiyaki is a taste experience like none other. They also offer delicious *chijimi*—this is the Japanese word for *jijim*, a delicious Korean dish similar in some ways to okonomiyaki that is often called *pajeon* in Korean. The friendly old ladies who run the place are welcoming, chatting with all of their customers. The prices at Takohachi are some of the lowest around, despite the quality of the food also being among the very best in town.

> Access: You can get to Takohachi from Tsuruhashi Station (Sennichimae Subway Line, JR Osaka Loop Line, Kintetsu lines). There is no easy way to describe how to get to Tsuruhashi,

so the best method is to go into the narrow shopping arcades in the area northeast of the three stations and simply ask somebody for directions (if you don't speak Japanese, be sure to point at the Japanese name and/or address listed in this entry while asking).

➢ Hours: 10:30 AM to 8:00 PM (until 6:00 PM on Sundays and public holidays). Closed on Wednesdays and the third Tuesday of each month.

➢ Phone: 06-6971-1781

➢ Japanese Address: 大阪市東成区東小橋 3-15-11

Ramen Guide

Osaka is widely known as a Japanese gourmet mecca, yet few people realize that it offers some of the best ramen around, including unique flavors that can't be found anywhere else.

The following is a list of recommended ramen shops in Osaka (in romanized alphabetical order), mostly located in Osaka City but in some cases located in the nearby suburbs. These suggestions are based on experience, recommendations, and Japanese-language ramen guides (I highly recommend the annual *Ramen Walker* guide). I have personally eaten at every ramen shop listed. I have also included a "Ramen Tutorial" for people who are not yet familiar with this delightful cuisine (instant ramen doesn't count).

Ramen Tutorial

Real ramen is a meal in itself, and unlike instant noodles, there is an art to making it. It is a hard dish to prepare well, and the combinations of ingredients and flavors are almost endless. Ramen varies greatly by region as well as by cook.

- **Broth:** The soup is the foundation of the ramen, and a ramen with bad broth cannot be considered good ramen. The four most common types of soup bases are *shoyu* (soy sauce), *miso*, *shio* (salt), and *tonkotsu* (pork-bone soup). While tonkotsu (most popular in Kyushu) is the most popular among most ramen lovers, the other flavors can be just as good or better when done right. There are many other soups, as well, including combinations of the above standard bases, chicken stock blends, and even *konbu* (kelp).

- **Noodles:** Noodles are another factor that can make or break a bowl of ramen, although average-tasting noodles can sometimes be partially compensated for by good soup and *chashu* pork. Noodles shipped in from a mass supplier tend to be the least impressive, while noodles hand-made in the shop (almost never the case with chain shops) are obviously the tastiest. Noodle thickness varies by shop and region. When you order, you can request hard, soft or regular noodles.

- **Toppings:** The most common toppings for ramen are *nori* (dried seaweed), *chashu* (thick, fatty pork slices), *kamaboko* (slices of fish cake), *moyashi* (bean sprouts), onions, green onions, *shinachiku* (seasoned bamboo shoots), mushrooms, *beni shoga* (red ginger strips pickled in *umezu*), and boiled eggs. Corn is occasionally added, and unexpected ingredients appear at less conventional shops—with ramen, anything goes. The quality of ingredients can drastically change the overall quality of the dish: a bad balance, poor-quality meat, or piles of cheap vegetables used to hide cheap noodles and bad broth can result in an unbearably awful bowl of ramen. On the other hand, a perfect blend of fine ingredients in the right amounts makes for some of the best food you've ever tasted.

- **Hot or cold (and *tsukemen*):** Ramen is often served hot, but there is also the option of eating *reimen*, which is very similar but served with cold noodles and cold soup in two separate dishes. Cold noodles really hit the spot during the hot, humid summer months in Osaka, when hot ramen may be too much to bear. When the noodles are separate from the soup, it is called *tsukemen*, in which case you dip the noodles in the soup before eating them.

- **How to eat:** Your ramen will come with a spoon and chopsticks, and there will be condiments such as garlic, ginger, *beni shoga*, sauces and spices on the counter in front of you. Add whatever you like, and sample the soup first if you want to by using the spoon. When you eat the noodles, use your chopsticks to bring them to your mouth, and then suck them in using your throat, rather than your lips—this is important, as using your throat (using lung power) will move the noodles down quickly and cool them as a result. It's perfectly normal to make slurping sounds when you eat ramen in Japan, and the abovementioned method usually produces such noises. After eating the noodles and toppings, it's also fine to pick up the bowl and drink the remaining soup directly from it. While many countries don't have such eating customs, there is no reason to feel self-conscious or nervous when doing these things in a Japan. People may even be impressed that you know how to eat like a local!

Ramen Shops

■ Chuka Soba Hanakyo (中華そば 花京)

This shop is located in the shopping arcade east of Kyobashi Station, and it is probably the best ramen you will find in Kyobashi (see p. 99 for more about the area). This tiny nine-seat shop has a big reputation, so expect to wait if you come during the lunch or dinner rush. The owner of Hanakyo used to be an ordinary company worker, but his dream of making the ideal ramen shop—a dream that started when he was a student—was always in the back of his mind, and after eight years of corporate life he quit to open his ramen shop. He has succeeded in creating a fun and lively shop with great food.

➤ Recommended: A basic bowl of tonkotsu *chashumen*.

➤ Access: 3–5 min. by foot from Kyobashi Station (JR lines, Keihan lines, Nagahori Tsurumi-ryokuchi Subway Line), but a little farther if you arrive on the JR Tozai Line or JR Gakkentoshi Line / Katamachi Line.

➤ Hours: 11:00 AM to 3:00 PM, 5:00 PM to 1:00 AM

➤ Phone: 06-6353-6620

➤ Japanese Address: 大阪市都島区東野田町 3-10-4

■ Hakata Ippudo (博多 一風堂)

Hakata Ippudo ramen, originally from Fukuoka (Kyushu), is popular nationwide, and it is a shop I have enjoyed since my days as a student in Tokyo. It has two unique tonkotsu broths—"red" and "white"—both of which are simply amazing (although I prefer "white" just a little more). The lunch set during the afternoon is a great deal and comes with ramen, *gyoza* and rice. You can also request noodle firmness in nine degrees from soft to hard.

➢ Recommended: Try both the red and white broths and choose your favorite. If you order ramen during lunchtime, you can pay an extra 100 yen to add rice and *gyoza* for an excellent and filling meal.

➢ Access: The most convenient shops are the Namba Shop (2–5 min. walk from Namba Station on any line except JR) and the Umeda Shop (5–7 min. walk from most Umeda stations / Osaka Station, located near Hankyu Higashidori (see p. 74)).

➢ Hours: Vary by shop, but generally 11:00 AM to 3:00 AM.

➢ Phone: 06-6363-3777 (Umeda), 06-4397-6886 (Namba)

➢ Japanese Address: 大阪市北区角田町 6-7 角田町ビル (Umeda), 大阪市浪速区難波中 3-1-17 (Namba)

■ Hokkaido Nagurikomi Ramen Betsubara (北海道なぐりこみ ラーメン 米通腹)

This is a small, family-run shop in a quiet residential neighborhood near Nishinagahori Subway Station. It serves refreshing, Hokkaido-style ramen with thick, filling noodles, richly flavored with a mixed *konbu*-and-tonkotsu broth. The number of bowls served is limited to a mere 100 per day!

➢ Recommended: Kiwamiso ramen, which uses miso broth and special sticky noodles made using Hokkaido potatoes.

➢ Access: 3 min. walk from exit 1 of Nishinagahori Station (Sennichimae and Nagahori Tsurumi-ryokuchi Subway Lines).

➢ Hours: Open from 11:30 AM to 3:00 PM and 5:00 PM to 10:00 PM on weekdays. Open from 11:30 AM to 10:00 PM on weekends.

➢ Phone: 06-6535-7218

➢ Japanese Address: 大阪市西区新町 3-7-5

■ Kinryu Ramen (金龍ラーメン)

What kind of Osakan would I be if I didn't mention Kinryu? This is the iconic ramen shop of Dotombori (see p. 49), and you can find shops all throughout the district. The keywords here are affordable, fast, and delicious. If you have been in Osaka for any length of time but haven't visited Kinryu, don't worry, I won't tell…but get there before somebody finds out! The simple ramen is extremely well-priced and shops are open almost any time of the day or night. You can recognize a Kinryu shop by the giant dragon on top.

➤ Recommended: A bowl of ramen here at 5:00 AM after a night of bar-hopping is bliss.

➤ Access: There are several Kinryu shops on Dotombori and around town, but the easiest one to find is along Midosuji Blvd. at the entrance to the Dotombori promenade (just a few steps from exit 14 of Namba Station on the Midosuji Subway Line).

➤ Hours: Vary by shop, but the Namba shops are open exceptionally late (including the one located on Midosuji Blvd.).

➤ Phone: 06-6211-3999

➤ Japanese Address: 大阪市中央区難波 1-7-13

■ Kyushu Ramen Kio (九州ラーメン亀王)

Kio (lit. "turtle king") is a ramen shop you will come across almost as often as Shi-Ten-Noh, and despite its name, it is a local Osaka chain. Its main attraction is the *chashumen*, which comes with thick, savory pieces of pork. This, in fact, is the main reason to go to Kio. I also recommend the refreshing *reimen* (cold ramen), which is even more delicious during Osaka's hot summers.

➤ Recommended: *Chashumen* is the best choice. Cool and refreshing *reimen* should be ordered instead during the hot summer months.

➤ Access: The Dotombori shop is about 5 min. on foot from Namba Station (Midosuji, Sennichimae and Yotsubashi Subway Lines, Kintetsu lines, Hanshin Namba Line, Nankai lines), the Kyobashi shop is about 5 min. on foot from Kyobashi Station

(Nagahori Tsurumi-ryokuchi Subway Line, JR lines, Keihan lines), and the Umeda shop is 1–2 min. on foot from Higashi-Umeda Station (Tanimachi Subway Line—near exit 7 from the subway line / exit H-82 from the underground shopping arcade) and not too far from the other Umeda Stations. There are many other shops around Osaka, too.

➢ Hours: Vary by shop, but most shops open at 11:00 AM and close between 3:30 AM and 5:00 AM.

➢ Phone: 06-6484-0090 (Dotombori (Namba)), 06-6353-9368 (Kyobashi), 06-6312-1616 (Umeda)

➢ Japanese Address: 大阪市中央区道頓堀 2-2-17 忠兵衛ビル 1F (Dotombori (Namba)), 大阪市都島区東野田町 5-2-23 (Kyobashi), 大阪市北区曾根崎 2-7-12 (Umeda)

■ Men'ya 7.5 Hz+ (麺屋 7.5Hz+)

While the name doesn't make much sense, the ramen is tasty enough that it doesn't have to. Ramen here is inexpensive and satisfying, and the restaurant has a unique layout made up of individual booths so you can feel comfortable even if you go alone. The soup has a rich, unique shoyu flavor.

➢ Recommended: The basic shoyu ramen for 600 yen is a good choice.

➢ Access: The Dotombori branch is located just 3 min. on foot from exit 2 of Nippombashi Station (Sakaisuji and Sennichimae Subway Lines, Kintetsu lines).

➢ Hours: 11:00 AM to 10:30 PM

➢ Phone: 06-6212-6616

➢ 大阪市中央区道頓堀 1-1-4 笑 POINT ビル B1F

■ Men'ya Eguchi (麺屋えぐち)

This tiny ramen shop, hidden away in a residential area near Esaka Station, is often packed with eager diners, the queue stretching out into the street. Its savory broth, scrumptious noodles and perfectly balanced flavor, not to mention the large volume of food you receive at a low price, makes it well worth the wait. This is possibly the best ramen shop I have come across in the northern Osaka suburbs.

➢ Recommended: Try the basic *tsukesoba*.

➢ Access: 5 min. walk from exit 1 of Esaka Station on the Kita-Osaka Kyuko Line (through services to this station operate from the Midosuji Subway Line).

➢ Hours: 11:00 AM to 2:30 AM, 6:00 AM to 11:00 PM (until 10:00 PM on Sundays and public holidays)

➢ Phone: 06-6338-0077

➢ Japanese Address: 大阪府吹田市江坂町 1-4-20

■ Men'ya Kurobune (麺屋 黒船)

The thing that surprised me the most about Kurobune wasn't the great set meal prices, the wide selection, or the member's card that gives customers a free side dish every time they come back—it was the miso ramen. Miso is a flavor that is hard to do well and often ends up tasting mediocre, but Kurobune's miso ramen is truly one of a kind. Men'ya Kurobune became one of my favorites in town after eating there the very first time. Try for yourself and become a believer!

➢ Recommended: The miso ramen is my top recommendation. The *shionegi-men*, with heaps of onions and a scrumptious broth, is also an excellent choice.

➢ Access: 1 min. walk from exit 4 of Yotsubashi Station (Yotsubashi Subway Line), which is connected via underground moving walkway to Shinsaibashi Station (Midosuji and Nagahori Tsurumi-ryokuchi Subway Lines).

➢ Hours: 11:00 AM to 2:00 AM (Monday to Thursday), but until 5:00 AM on Fridays and Saturdays, and until midnight on Sundays and public holidays.

➢ Phone: 06-6531-0241

➢ Japanese Address: 大阪市西区北堀江 1-6-5 欧州館 1F

■ Shi-Ten-Noh (四天王)

While Shi-Ten-Noh offers good quality ramen in tonkotsu-shio, tonkotsu-shoyu and tonkotsu-miso flavors, it's worth coming here just to try the tonkotsu-shio. The *chashu* pork and noodles are average but the soup tastes superb, and for a chain restaurant everything is fairly good and prices are low. Plus, finding truly tasty shio ramen is a rare and beautiful thing, because shio is rarely taken as seriously as shoyu or tonkotsu. Be sure to give this local ramen chain a try during your time in Osaka.

➤ Recommended: The tonkotsu-shio *chashumen* is a sure choice.

➤ Access: While there are Shi-Ten-Nohs all over the city, the most convenient ones are probably those in Namba. The Namba-naka Shop is located about 2 min. on foot from Nankai Namba Station; the Sennichimae Shop is located within 5 min. on foot from both Nippombashi Station and Namba Station; and the Dotombori Shop is located right along the Dotombori promenade (see p. 49), 5 min. on foot from Namba Station. There is also a shop near Nakatsu Station on the Tanimachi Subway Line, just one stop from Umeda.

➤ Hours: Vary by shop, but most are open from 11:00 AM to 2:00 or 3:00 AM.

➤ Phone: 06-6633-8808 (Namba-naka), 06-6649-3372 (Sennichi-mae), 06-6212-6350 (Dotombori), 06-6375-7815 (Nakatsu)

➤ Japanese Address: 大阪市浪速区難波中 1-18-8 大阪開発難波ビル (Namba-naka), 大阪市中央区千日前 2-11-4 (Sennichimae), 大阪市中央区道頓堀 1-7-25 タカコ第五ビル (Dotombori), 大阪市北区豊崎 5-7-5 第 2 北梅田ビル 1F (Nakatsu)

■ Sodaisho (総大醤)

Even though I listed the ramen shops in alphabetical order to avoid bias, the best has coincidentally been saved for last in this ramen guide—Osaka's shoyu ramen is some of the best I have tasted in Japan, and Sodaisho is by far my favorite place to eat it. This famous little shop has lines that stretch out the door, and its specialty is an incredibly rich and flavorful shoyu broth. Television stars and celebrities often come here to dine. The *chashu-don*, which is a *donburi*-style dish with rice, mayonnaise, *nori* and *chashu* pork, is nothing short of wonderful. For shoyu ramen in Osaka, there is no better place than Sodaisho.

➢ Recommended: *Shoyu chashumen* and *chashu-don* make for a delicious and filling meal.

➢ Access: The most popular shop is a 4 min. walk from exit 11 of Tenjimbashisuji 6-chome Station (Tanimachi and Sakaisuji Subway Lines, Hankyu Senri Line).

➢ Hours: 11:00 AM to 3:00 PM, 5:30 PM to midnight

➢ Phone: 06-6375-8260

➢ Japanese Address: 大阪市北区浮田 2-4-16

Festivals and Events

There are a variety of festivals and events throughout the year that can make your time in Osaka more exciting. I have outlined some of the main ones that take place every year (listed in chronological order).

■ Toka Ebisu (十日戎)—Winter

A festival just after the start of the new year, Toka Ebisu has been around for hundreds of years, and the Toka Ebisu in Osaka is said to be the biggest in Japan with approximately one million people attending over three days. Ebisu is a deity who supposedly grants wealth and good fortune in business and commerce, so many businesspeople visit Imamiya-Ebisu Shrine (see p. 125) for this festival. Bamboo branches with various charms attached are sold to festival-goers who buy them for good luck, and handed over by lovely young women wearing *yukata*. Geisha are carried through the streets on palanquins, and there is even a coal-walking event. And of course, food stalls of every sort are put out and lanterns are strung up all the way from Shin-Imamiya to Namba.

> When: January 9–11 (the main event is on January 10).

> Where: Imamiya-Ebisu Shrine (see p. 125), which is a short walk from Ebisucho Station on the Sakaisuji Subway Line and Hankai Streetcar Line, and Imamiyaebisu Station on the Nankai Koya Line (only local trains stop here).

■ Doya Doya (どやどや)—Winter

Doya Doya is held at Shitennoji Temple (see p. 109) at the end of Shushoue, a Buddhist ritual starting on January 1st that revolves around prayers for peace and rich harvests. Men of all ages clad in small loincloths—the reason this is known as one of the biggest "naked man" festivals of Japan—are splashed with water in the middle of winter, and they scramble for banknotes in front of the temple.

➤ When: January 14, from 2:00 PM to 4:00 PM.

➤ Where: Doya Doya is held at Shitennoji Temple (see p. 109), near Shitennoji-mae Yuhigaoka Station on the Tanimachi Subway Line. Admission to the temple is free for this event, although certain parts of the temple (such as the treasure hall) cost extra.

■ **Cherry Blossoms at the Japan Mint Building in Osaka (大阪 造幣局の花見)—Spring**

The Osaka Mint Building is the best place to see cherry blossoms in Osaka City. Since the nineteenth century, the Mint has continued its tradition of opening its garden to the public for one week a year when its cherry blossoms are in full bloom. There are about 350 trees of 120 varieties, and they are even illuminated during the evening to create a beautifully surreal spectacle. Although 350 is a relatively small number of trees compared to other famous cherry blossom spots, the beauty and variety of these carefully tended trees is what makes them so famous.

➤ When: The schedule changes every year depending on the weather and state of the cherry blossoms. The only way to confirm the dates with certainty is to look on the Mint's website (see below). There are also ads listing dates posted around Temmabashi Station prior to the event.

➤ Where: From Temmabashi Station (Tanimachi Subway Line, Keihan lines), walk north across the bridge (outside of exit 1 or 2 of the subway station, or the east exit of the Keihan station). When you reach the opposite bank, you will see the entrance and the crowds of people heading toward the Mint grounds.

➤ Additional Information: http://www.mint.go.jp/eng/index.html

■ Tenjin Matsuri (天神祭)—Summer

This is one of the three biggest festivals in Japan and the biggest in Osaka by far, with a history of more than 1,000 years and millions of people attending each year. The precession starts at Tenmangu Shrine (see p. 92), proceeding first over land and then over the waters of the Okawa River for the grand finale. Riders of the festival boats dance to the hypnotic beats of the Japanese percussion instruments while one of Osaka's biggest fireworks displays lights up the sky above. Over 3,000 people work together using more than 100 boats to throw this festival, and *yukata*-clad viewers line the banks of the river to watch, drinking beer and eating scrumptious snacks sold from nearby food stalls (*yatai*). *Bunraku* (puppet theatre) performances also take place throughout town. If you only see one festival in Osaka, Tenjin Matsuri is the best choice.

➢ When: Late afternoon on July 24 (at Tenmangu Shrine) and starting in the evening on July 25 (along the Okawa River). The latter is a must-see.

➢ Where: Tenmangu Shrine (near Minami-morimachi Station on the Sakaisuji and Tanimachi Subway Lines, and Osaka-temmangu Station on the JR Tozai Line—see see p. 92) and the Okawa River (near Temmabashi Station on the Tanimachi Subway Line and Keihan lines) are the central areas for this event.

➢ Additional Information: http://www.osaka-info.jp/tenjin _matsuri/main_en.html

■ Sumiyoshi Matsuri (住吉祭)—Summer

This festival takes place in late July and early August, and features a number of unique events including the Nagoshi-Harai-Shinji ritual in which women and children dress in Muromachi Period costumes and pass through a large ring, and a portable shrine precession from Sumiyoshi Grand Shrine in Osaka City (see p. 124) to Shukuin Tongu Shrine in Sakai City.

➢ When: July 30 to August 1

➢ Where: Sumiyoshi Grand Shrine (see p. 124), which is directly in front of Sumiyoshi Torii-mae Station on the Hankai Streetcar Line, or a 3 min. walk from Sumiyoshitaisha Station on the Nankai main line.

■ Naniwa Yodogawa Fireworks Festival (なにわ淀川花火大会)—Summer

One of the biggest and most popular fireworks festivals in Osaka, the Naniwa Yodogawa Fireworks Festival has been held next to the Shin-Yodogawa River every year since 1989, and despite its large scale, the festival is conducted almost entirely by the local residents and businesses of the Juso area (see p. 77). Attendance each year is approximately 500,000, and the fireworks display is massive. Many people come dress in *yukata*, so it's a good chance to try wearing one of your own!

➢ When: The festival is held on the first Saturday of August every year. The fireworks are launched from 7:50 PM and the show continues until around 9:00 PM, but unless you have a reserved seat somewhere, I suggest bringing your tarp or blanket and staking out a place along the river in the afternoon so you will have somewhere to sit at night.

➢ Where: It is held along the riverbanks of the Shin-Yodogawa River in the Juso area (see p. 77). The closest train stations are Juso Station on the Hankyu Kobe, Takarazuka and Kyoto Lines, and Tsukamoto Station on the JR Kobe Line (only local trains stop here). It is also possible to walk to the venue from the Umeda area.

➢ Additional Information: http://www.yodohanabi.com (Japanese only)

■ Kishiwada Danjiri Matsuri (岸和田だんじり祭)—Autumn

Danjiri festivals are cart-pulling festivals held in various locales throughout Japan, but the Kishiwada Danjiri Festival is arguably the most famous—or perhaps infamous, since participants tend to get hurt often. Huge festival floats on wheels, known as *danjiri*, are raced through the narrow streets at blistering speeds by large teams of *happi*-coat-clad participants holding ropes on all sides that are thrown about by whiplash during sharp turns—pieces of buildings are sometimes broken off when a *danjiri* team navigates a turn poorly. There is also a man with a fan dancing to the beats of traditional percussion instruments on top of the slanted roof of the fast-moving *danjiri*. The floats themselves are works of art, with intricate woodwork and ornate decorations (also see p. 143). Despite the dangers of this festival, it is a treasured Kishiwada tradition dating back to 1703.

➤ When: There are actually two Danjiri Matsuri in the Kishiwada area, with the more famous of the two being held in September, and the other being held in October. The more famous one is held on the mornings of the Saturday and Sunday preceding Respect for the Aged Day (third Monday of September).

➤ Where: The September festival starts near Nankai Kishiwada Station and runs toward the seaside, while the October festival is held near Nankai Haruki Station (both stations are on the Nankai main line).

■ Osaka Hikari-Renaissance (OSAKA 光のルネサンス)— Winter

The holiday season is a time for romance in Japan, so this Christmas light display event is the perfect chance to take someone special out for a walk by the rivers and stately old buildings of Nakanoshima (see p. 81). It can also be fun for expats who miss the holiday spirit of home. Aside from the lights, there is a large Christmas tree on display, choirs singing, and a musical performance with amazing visuals projected on the wall of the Osaka Prefectural Nakanoshima Library (don't miss this!). Food stalls are also set up in Nakanoshima Park and along the riverbanks, and special boats tours in vessels decorated for the holidays are available during the event period.

➤ When: For about two weeks from early or mid-December until December 25, generally from 5:00 to 10:00 PM (varies by individual event). Before these dates, a portion of the lights are usually lit up.

➢ Where: Most of the lights and events are on Nakanoshima (see p. 81). If you are taking the subway, the best place to get off is Yodoyabashi Station on the Midosuji Subway Line or Kitahama Station on the Sakaisuji Subway Line. If you are taking Keihan, it's best to get off at Yodoyabashi or Kitahama Station on the Keihan Main Line, or Oebashi or Naniwabashi Station on the Keihan Nakanoshima Line. There are also some light displays near Temmabashi Station (Keihan lines and Tanimachi Subway Line), Higobashi Station (Yotsubashi Subway Line), and Nakanoshima Station (Keihan Nakanoshima Line). Additionally, lights are put up near Osaka Aquarium Kaiyukan (see p. 115).

➢ Additional Information: http://www.osaka-hikari.com/index _eng.html

The Meaning of Travel

I am not sure how or when I became a travel addict. Certainly there is an allure in going to new places, encountering unpredictable situations, and seeing unfamiliar things, but understanding where that feeling comes from takes a bit more thinking. Upon reflection, this is what I came up with.

To start with, I think the opportunity to escape from daily worries was a major reason. Whether we know it or not, every day is filled with anxiety about trifling things that needn't be worried about in the first place. As I pore over documents each day, wracking my brain for new ad copy, elegant translations and smoother rewrites, I become physically and mentally exhausted. After work I worry about what I need to do, what I haven't done, what can't be done but should be done. The amount of things to do in a day is simply overwhelming. However, the moment I step foot on the train or bus bound for my next travel destination, all of that is forgotten. Whether it be a day- or a week-long excursion, the time is my time, and I can think about things like the future, my humanity, the world around me, and the little things that often go unnoticed—things I don't have time to consider on most days. The lack of small worries enables me to finally see the world clearly.

Then there is one of the most basic concepts in travel: movement. I firmly believe that movement, both literally and figuratively, is freedom. I always bring along books to read on my train trips, but in the end only about five pages or so ever get read, because I just stare out the window at the things gliding by—at scenery both familiar and new. Just the ability to move, whether it be at a screaming Shinkansen speed or rickety *wanman* clunker-train crawl (see photo below), is exhilarating. It's no coincidence that we say life is "at a standstill" when things seem to be stagnant and unchanging; movement, whether it be toward something or just for movement's sake, is liberating.

Movement also means we are going to new places and seeing new things. But why is that important? Because encountering new situations, people, and ideas helps us grow, especially when we don't have the burden of everyday worries weighing us down and hindering clear thinking. I have never gone on a trip and come back the same person: whether it was to a small or large degree, I have always changed and grown through travel. My view of the world changes and my perspective expands and becomes more refined. Traveling alone sometimes enhances these aspects further.

So get out there and explore, see everything you can while there is still time. Enjoy not only the destination, but the journey to get there. Appreciate small things, and don't plan every day meticulously. Go somewhere nobody  would ever think of taking a trip to, stay somewhere—a run-down hostel, a capsule hotel, a sleeping bag under the stars—you wouldn't normally stay. Take every type of trip you can, at any chance you can get, and you will not only experience more of the world, but will become a happier person with a richer set of experiences to look back on.

A free mind, movement, growth, and new experiences. Together, these are the meaning of travel.

First photograph: The Seto Inland Sea from Onomichi, Hiroshima Prefecture.
Second photograph: A rural train on the Yosan Line at Iyo-Ozu Station in Ehime Prefecture, south of Matsuyama.

Creating Life Experiences: How to Get the Most Out of Your Travel

I first published this on my Osaka Insider *blog (http://osakainsider .wordpress.com) in early 2010. While some of this applies only to rural travel (such as in southern Osaka Prefecture), most of it applies to urban travel as well.*

This is a list of personal recommendations, based on my own travel experiences and the advice of others (professional and otherwise). Many of them apply to travel in general. Following these tips will help you experience life-changing journeys and discover more about the world and about yourself.

- **Travel cheap**: This is not just a budgeting tip. Traveling cheap enables you see the things Japanese people see, and following more conventional routes reveals the "real" Japan that you might otherwise miss. I personally do not recommend bus tours and the like run by big companies, unless you want the adult version of an elementary-school field trip. In fact, packaged tours are usually more expensive and less fun than tours you can plan yourself by doing a little research.

- **...but don't plan everything**: In other words, leave room for the unexpected. A trip where everything goes as planned is like visiting Chinatown and saying you went to China. Research travel times and locations, and create a reasonable schedule of things you want to see each day, as well as a list of other things you might want to see. But more importantly, do not feel the need to stick to that schedule all the time. If something down a side street catches your eye as you walk, go take a look. If you want to linger at the Zen garden and ponder your thoughts an hour longer, do it. Trying to orchestrate an experience too closely causes it to lose its natural flow and become superficial.

- **Try things you wouldn't otherwise do**: Especially if you are an introvert, this is a perfect chance to try things you wouldn't otherwise do. Nobody knows you there, and you do not live there, so try coming out of your shell and allow the experience change you. Travel is not just about seeing something new, but about letting yourself grow. Note that I am not recommending doing anything indecent, illegal, obnoxious or rude—don't forget to use common sense, and don't forget that you are a guest in Japan.

- **Forget what's going on at home**: You will get the most out of your experience if you leave your worries and daily concerns behind (this includes checking e-mail, updating blogs, etc.). Use the chance to not only relax, but immerse yourself fully in a fascinating new world.

- **Stay awake on trains**: Some of the most beautiful and interesting sights you see will be from the train window. Get enough sleep in the hotel and stay awake on the train (or bus).

- **Rent a bicycle**: Particularly in rural areas, getting around by bicycle enables you to see hidden things you would never have had the chance to see otherwise. It also gives you more opportunities to meet interesting people. And of course, exercise never hurts. Bicycle rentals are cheap, and shops are generally easy to find near train stations.

- **Don't just hit tourist traps**: I recommend going to small attractions or simply roaming around without a purpose every once and a while. The best experiences I have had came from walking down random streets, taking small side paths, and visiting small, family-run restaurants and shops.

- **Try to speak Japanese**: The ability to speak the language of the country you are visiting enhances the experience by a huge degree. By speaking only English, you are limiting yourself to what has been translated and people who can speak English, which means you are not seeing Japan for what it really is. If you are visiting as a tourist, take a few weeks to study beforehand or try out a few guidebook phrases when you have the opportunity—even if your Japanese is terrible, people here will praise you lavishly for your "excellent" language skills. Disillusion yourself of the belief that everyone in the world knows English and nobody minds having to use it. It's more considerate to at least try to speak the country's language and respect its culture, as opposed to expecting them to accommodate you.

- **Eat local specialty foods**: Every region of Japan and most cities and towns have their own specialty foods. You will not only get a wide sampling of Japanese cuisine, but you will have a richer travel experience if you try local specialties along the way. It also makes picking a menu item simple!

- **Go out drinking**: There are few better ways to meet and talk to locals than sharing drinks with them. Research local bars if possible before setting out on your journey (WikiTravel is a good resource for this: http://wikitravel.org), and follow the recommendations of other expats in Japan.

- **Stay at an *onsen* (hot spring)**: I know it's probably scary to think of being naked in front of complete strangers, but hot spring baths are one of the most wonderful parts of Japan, and they can be found almost everywhere (even in central Osaka City—see p. 102). Schedule one night at a hotel, *ryokan*, or resort with hot spring baths (or even just regular shared baths) and enjoy yourself—outdoor baths in the autumn and winter are particularly lovely. Some hotels have *kashikiri-buro*, which are baths that can be reserved for private use.

Photograph: A canal in Omihachiman, Shiga Prefecture.

Why I Live Here

I first published this on my Osaka Insider *blog (http://osakainsider .wordpress.com) in early 2010.*

I am often asked what I like about living in Osaka. And because I have also lived in Tokyo, I am also asked whether I prefer Osaka or Tokyo. Besides the fact that my job and life are here, there are four primary reasons I prefer to live in Osaka over any other place in Japan:

1. The People

This is the number one reason Osaka is one of the most livable places I have found in Japan. People here are extremely open-minded (including their attitudes toward foreign residents), are willing to help out strangers, and are basically warm and approachable. It is easy to strike up a conversation with a stranger almost anywhere you go, and if you need help because you are lost or unsure of something, just ask someone nearby and you will almost always receive help. This "people" factor is my reason for staying here, and also the reason cited by numerous others.

2. Livability

With a population of nearly 3 million, Osaka City is big but not too big, and despite the tri-city metro area population of approximately 20 million, it does not (for the most part) have the hellish commutes, snail-like traffic and infuriating crowds of larger cities like Tokyo.

There are many small shops and businesses mixed in with department stores and chain stores, so you can easily find something that suites your tastes—the inexhaustible number of hidden places to explore is one of the city's best features. Unlike its historical rival, Tokyo, Osaka is planned well, so you won't get lost wandering the streets. The cost of living is also more than reasonable in comparison. Finally, Osaka has many well-designed parks and waterfront spots, making for a pleasant urban environment. Despite its past reputation as a dirty, industrial city, Osaka has become a massive commercial center and one of the cleanest and most livable cities you will find.

3. Rich Culture and History

Osaka has played many roles throughout its history, including that of the imperial capital (as Naniwa-kyo), an important trade port and point for importing cultural innovations, a diplomatic host for Chinese and Korean visitors after the capital moved first to Nara and then Kyoto, the base of Toyotomi military power, the prime economic center and site of the world's first futures exchange during the Edo Period (1600–1868), a major manufacturing center during the early modern period and period of high-speed growth, a temporary capital when Tokyo was burned to the ground in the fires of the 1923 earthquake, a primary commercial and trade center since the postwar period, and now an increasingly international city and central hub for Japan and East Asia. This rich history has given rise to a unique culture and a number of rich, deep-rooted traditions. Osaka is also the central transportation hub of Kansai, so you can reach places such as Nara, Kyoto and Himeji in no time.

4. The Food

Osaka is historically known as "the nation's kitchen" for its role in supplying and acting as a hub for the food-supply industries. It is also famous for its cuisine—not luxury cuisine, mind you, but down-to-earth dishes. The quality of *okonomiyaki* (see p. 159)*, takoyaki,* ramen (see p. 163)*, soba, kushikatsu* (see p. 103), sushi, and other such foods is outstanding. In addition, the large number of non-Japanese living in the city means there is a huge selection of international cuisine (Korean food in Tsuruhashi, for example—see p. 105). Delicious food at surprisingly low prices is definitely one of the city's strongest points.

Photograph: Scene from the Toka Ebisu festival in Osaka (see p. 175).

Sakai: Kansai's Lost City

I can't count the number of times I have heard overseas visitors and nationals complaining about the tragic loss of traditional Kyoto. It was one of the few major cities in Japan to be spared bombing of any sort at the end of World War II, and the fact that the old wooden buildings and roadways are mostly gone is due to rapid urban development.

But I don't think that Kyoto is the great tragedy of Kansai. I don't even think that it has really been lost, as most of its culture and traditions are still intact, its arts are still practiced, and it is respected as the cultural center of Japan by almost all, despite the considerable legacies of places such as Edo and Osaka. And regardless of its considerable size and the laws that make preservation of wooden structures difficult, Kyoto has still managed to maintain a significant amount of its architectural legacy. The real tragedy of Kansai is the city of Sakai, which has become a dreary southern-Osaka suburb and a manufacturing center. Urbanization and modernization have not only created a city that is, for the most part, run-down and depressing, they have chiseled away at the cultural legacy of Sakai to such a degree that most Japanese don't even know of the city's importance in Japanese history and culture.

One of the more well-known facts about Sakai is that it has historically produced the best-quality blades in Japan and most consider it to be one of the great centers of blade production (mostly cutlery in modern times) in the entire world. Sakai swords will set you back nearly a life savings, and genuine swords today are considered national treasures, and thus cannot be legally taken out of the country. Sakai was also a pioneer of early bicycle manufacturing in Japan, and even now produces a large amount of Japan's bicycles. There are many crafts still done by hand in Sakai, including dying of cloth, painting of *koi-nobori* (Sakai is one of the rare places where this is still done by hand), and wood carving.

And let's not forget one of the most influential cultural legacies to come of out Sakai, the tea master Sen no Rikyu, who was history's most influential figure in developing and solidifying the art of the Japanese tea ceremony—he was important enough to be the personal tea master of both Oda Nobunaga and Toyotomi Hideyoshi, two of history's greatest shoguns and rulers. Sen no Rikyu was held in such high esteem that he helped host a tea ceremony for the emperor and was bestowed with an honorary title as a result. And if Sen no Rikyu isn't enough to impress you, try opening Google Maps and taking a look at some of the largest ancient imperial tombs in existence (in carefully executed keyhole shapes, some large enough to be seen from space—also see p. 136), which are scattered here and there throughout Sakai City. When excavated, these tombs contained some of the most valuable artifacts from ancient Japan that have been found, revealing a massive amount of information about ancient Japanese history, art, culture and lifestyles. And the reason these tombs are in Sakai? Because that region is where the emperors first reigned over Japan, long before Nara and then Kyoto became the capitals in the late eighth century AD.

Sakai started as a fishing village—many of the temples and shrines, including the impressive Sumiyoshi Grand Shrine, are dedicated to deities said to ensure safe sea travel. It later developed into a merchant town, much like its bigger neighbor Osaka, except that in the case of Sakai it was an autonomous, self-governed body (a "free city," or 自由都市)—this was also the case with other cities in Japan at the time, including the thriving merchant town of Hakata in Kyushu. It was during this time that Sakai's skilled crafts and arts, which are still around today, began to develop rapidly. Sakai was also growing into an important trade hub during this time (mostly domestic trade). Around the time of the Meiji Restoration (1868), Japan was following a similar path of "modernization" to that of Europe and the United States, but it had to industrialize more quickly in order to keep up with the world's other top powers and avoid falling prey to imperialism. This meant that cities like Sakai grew quickly, and factories started sprouting up here and there, polluting the air and making for the start of what would come to be a dreadful cityscape. Like many other cities, Sakai was firebombed by allied forces (mostly American) near the end of World War II, and much of the city was destroyed. The postwar period of high-speed growth in Japan led to further industrial development of Sakai, and today there are many large artificial islands filling the bay. Although it is better than in recent years, Sakai has not seen the shift toward a commercial (rather than industrial) economy as Osaka has, and smoke and sulfurous smells still fill the air near the bay.

Today, Sakai aims to become a model environmental city for Japan, and the national and local governments have put money and effort into achieving this ideal. Promising projects, such as the collaborative solar plant and factory recently built by Sharp and Kansai Electric Power, do make it seem as if real progress is being made, but a visit to the city makes it painfully clear that Sakai still has decades (at least) before it can revert back to being a cultural icon and more livable city. Personally, I don't think building more is the answer; I think reducing polluting industries, expanding transportation infrastructure, enhancing technologies to cut down on pollution, and attracting non-polluting businesses will be a start toward the model "green city" goal. The building of a new national (and international) soccer training facility in Sakai is seen by some as a promising new direction, especially considering its convenient location near Osaka City and Kansai International Airport.

Sakai has also made strong efforts to promote tourism in recent years, including printing sightseeing-related materials, and I want to join in that promotion effort as well (independently of any affiliation, of course). Sakai is a friendly city with a fascinating and unique history, and many of its older citizens are struggling to keep its fading culture and customs alive despite disinterest among youth. Considering how tough things have been for the tourism industry after the March 2011 earthquakes and tsunamis, and also the fact that Sakai is located right next door to bigger attractions such as Kyoto, Nara, and Osaka, it's not going to be an easy fight. But for those of you who want to delve deeper and see a more unique side of Japan, take a look at the Sakai section starting on p. 134.

Let's not let this unique and fascinating gem of Japan slip away through negligence. I truly hope that Sakai, a casualty of development and centralization, will one day return to its former glory. At the very least, I hope it will not be forgotten.

Photograph: The old lighthouse of Sakai, Osaka (see p. 139) is seen on the right, nearly eclipsed by a tangle of elevated expressways.

In Defense of Shin-Imamiya, Shinsekai and Nishinari

Shin-Imamiya, Shinsekai and Nishinari—these three places are considered by people throughout Kansai as dangerous. Many guidebooks parrot the same mindless hearsay, advising people to not even set foot in these neighborhoods. However, their reputation for being "dangerous" is undeserved, or at least highly exaggerated.

Let's start with Shinsekai, the home of Tsutenkaku (see p. 103), Spa World (see p. 102), and some of Osaka's best *fugu* (blowfish) and *kushikatsu* restaurants. The area has a reputation for being "dangerous," but in all seriousness, there is almost nothing dangerous here. People talk about *yakuza*[7] presence, but this has been gone for decades. Of course, it is not the kind of place a woman would want to walk through alone at night, but for the most part it just smells bad because of all the homeless people living in the covered shopping arcades.

Then there is Shin-Imamiya, the awful-looking, foul-smelling area at the bottom of the JR Osaka Loop Line, near the Airin labor center. There are many homeless people and generally creepy people,

---

[7] The *yakuza* are the leading Japanese organized crime group in the country. Some English-language literature refers to the *yakuza* as the "Japanese mafia."

but there is minimal danger in this station-front area. It is actually a popular place for backpackers and budget travelers from abroad to stay, as many of the *doya*[8] that day laborers used to live in have been converted to extremely cheap hotels and hostels (2,000 yen or so a night) and the location is convenient for sightseeing in and around Osaka as well as for nights out in Minami. The day laborers themselves are, for the most part, not bad people—many of them were workers who fell victim to economic downturn, members of outcast groups, or else "salarymen" and the like who couldn't cut it in corporate life and had no families to support them after losing their jobs. Of course there are also alcoholics, criminals, and the like mixed in, but that's definitely not the norm (despite what some people will tell you). An interesting bit of Shin-Imamiya culture: on the south side of the JR station and west of the Nankai tracks, at around 5:00 AM or so on most mornings, homeless, poor, and regular residents of the area hold a flea market, selling all sorts of interesting things they pick up from around town. While there's nothing there really worth buying, it's fun to browse through.

Lastly, there's Nishinari, of which Shin-Imamiya is a part. This ward became infamous in 1991 when the Nishinari Riots occurred, stemming from dissatisfaction on the part of day laborers and homeless in the area and also in response to unfair (and sometimes brutal) treatment by police. This sort of violence rarely occurs on such a large scale in Japan, a country that is considered extremely safe, and as a result Nishinari came into the spotlight as a "dangerous place." Now, I will admit that Nishinari is not a very nice part of town by any means, and it really isn't a very good place to live, but for the most part it's safe as long as you know where to go and where not to go. (Tip: Stay out of the southeast area.)

---

[8] *Doya* (ドヤ) is a slang term used by day laborers for facilities where small rooms can be rented out for short- or long-term stays. These facilities are used by many day laborers who stay when they have enough money (or when the weather is too cold), and sleep outside at other times. The term comes from the common word *yado*, which means home or lodging, but with the two Japanese letters *ya* and *do* put in reverse order (宿→ヤ ド→ドヤ). In order to stay in business amid decreases in the day laborer population, owners of many *doya* have converted their facilities into hostels targeting backpackers from abroad and other budget travelers.

I spent about two years living in these areas (one year in Ebisucho just a short walk from Shin-Imamiya and right next to Shinsekai, and one year in Nishinari itself on the other side of Shin-Imamiya), so I have seen both the good and the bad. These are poorer parts of town, but I truly think their reputation for being extremely dangerous is exaggerated, although their reputation for being filthy and dirty is spot-on. Even though these areas are probably less safe than other parts of town, a little common sense is all you need to avoid trouble. Perhaps my attitude is related to my different perception of what is "dangerous," having grown up visiting American cities where real danger is more commonly encountered.

Furthermore, there really is a sense of community in these areas, whether it be in the Shinsekai neighborhood (an old neighborhood where people take pride in their history), among the homeless and day laborers, or among the many non-Japanese and other people who don't quite fit in to society as a "normal" Japanese person might.

Photograph: Tsutenkaku (see p. 103) at night.

Osaka City Subway Map

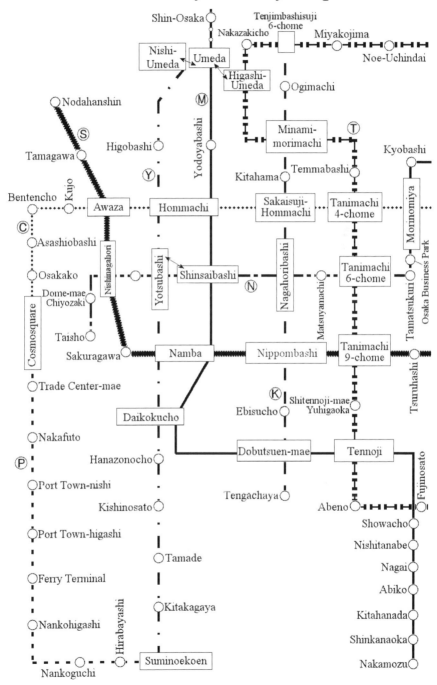

Note: This is only a partial map of the Osaka subway system (the Imazato Line to the east is not included). Square stations represent stations shared by more than one subway line, and arrows between two square stations with different names (for example, Yotsubashi/Shinsaibashi and Nishi-Umeda/Umeda/Higashi-Umeda) means they are considered to be the same station, so you can transfer between lines.

This map is not to scale, and it does not indicate true directions and distances—it is only for navigating the subway system.

Spellings (romanizations) are the same as those used on the Osaka Municipal Transportation Bureau's website, which should match what is written in the actual stations themselves.

I have used a different line pattern for each subway line, and I have also added symbols (letters enclosed in circles) to indicate which line is which. The following letters correspond to the following lines:

Ⓜ   Midosuji Line

Ⓣ   Tanimachi Line

Ⓨ   Yotsubashi Line

Ⓒ   Chuo Line

Ⓢ   Sennichimae Line

Ⓚ   Sakaisuji Line

Ⓝ   Nagahori Tsurumi-ryokuchi Line

Ⓟ   Nanko Port Town Line / New Tram Line

JR Osaka Loop Line Map

The JR Tozai and Sakurajima/Yumesaki Lines are also shown, as are portions of other JR lines. Dotted lines are private rail lines. Subway Lines are not shown. For a full rail line overview, visit http://www.osaka-info.jp/en/access/info_train.html.

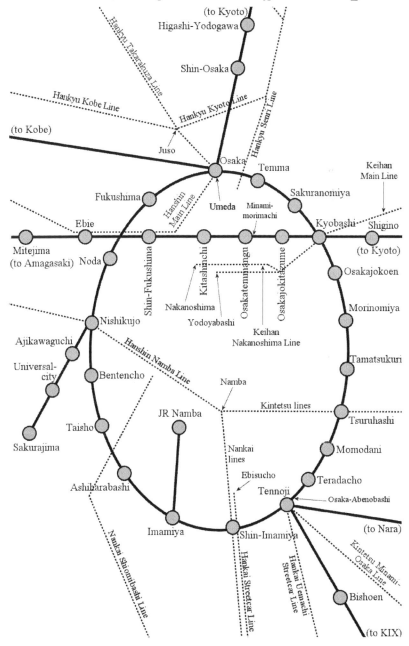

Yodoyabashi Area Walking Map

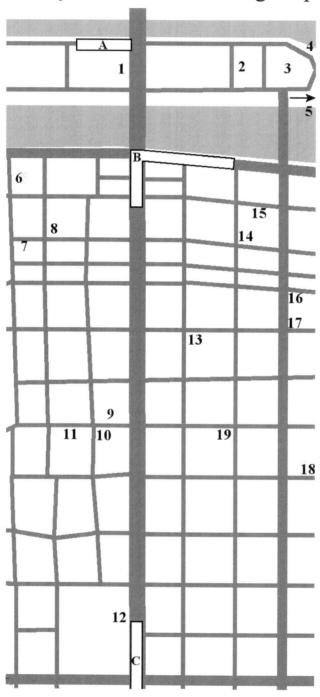

Kitahama Area Walking Map

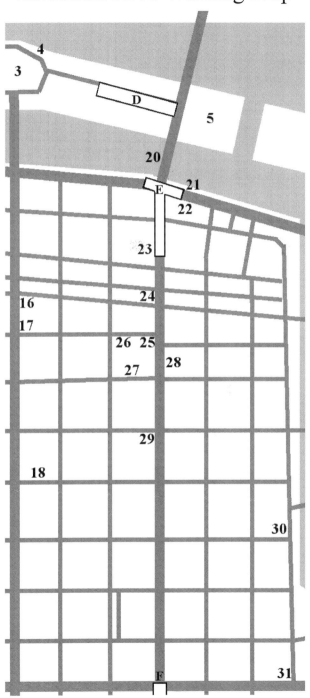

Yodoyabashi and Kitahama Walking Maps

A. Oebashi Station (Keihan Nakanoshima Line)

B. Yodoyabashi Station (Midosuji Subway Line, Keihan Main Line)

C. Hommachi Station (Midosuji, Chuo and Yotsubashi Subway Lines)

D. Naniwabashi Station (Keihan Nakanoshima Line)

E. Kitahama Station (Sakaisuji Subway Line, Keihan Main Line)

F. Sakaisuji-Hommachi Station (Chuo and Sakaisuji Subway Lines)

1. Bank of Japan (Osaka Branch): The Osaka branch of the Bank of Japan was built in 1903 by Kingo Tatsuno, the same architect who built the Kokaido building and Tokyo Station. Although it is not the primary branch of the Bank, it is the most architecturally beautiful incarnation and acts as the Bank's primary visual symbol. (See photograph on p. 26.)

2. Osaka Prefectural Nakanoshima Library: This lovely building was built in 1904 and displays some of the city's most elegant Meiji Period (1868–1912) architecture. The left and right wings were added later. Valuable historical texts on Osaka can be viewed inside.

3. Kokaido: Osaka City Central Public Hall, often referred to as Kokaido, was completed in 1918. This flashy retro building is the symbol of Nakanoshima and a famous landmark in Osaka. Its architecture screams Meiji, and at night its Neo-Renaissance design looks even more impressive thanks to masterful illumination. There is a retro cafe on the basement level (very affordable during lunchtime, more expensive for dinner).

4. The Museum of Oriental Ceramics, Osaka: See p. 84.

5. Nakanoshima Park: See p. 85.

6. Former Sumitomo Building: One of the most impressive retro buildings in Kitahama, the two sections of this building were finished in 1926 and 1930. It truly displays the power and influence of Sumitomo.

7. **Former Imabashi Branch Station of Chuo Fire Brigade:** Originally built in 1925, this lovely little building is now used as a restaurant.

8. **Osaka Club:** Completed in 1912, this brick building has a certain subdued charm and refinement to it. Still used for upscale events, it was designed as a gentlemen's club (modeled after the British custom) for prominent Osakans at the time.

9. **Osaka Gas Building:** Built in 1933 and still in use as the headquarters of Osaka Gas, this is one of Midosuji Blvd.'s grandest buildings. During World War II, its metal parts were removed and melted down to assist wartime manufacturing efforts.

10. **Kitano Residence:** Completed in 1928, this was the residence of local merchant Eitaro Kitano. Although most of the neighborhood was destroyed during the bombings of World War II, this residence miraculously remained standing.

11. **Goryo Shrine:** The shrine's history dates back to the ninth century, and in more modern times, it was a center of *bunraku* puppet theatre culture (a famous Osaka tradition—see p. 63). It provides shade and a quiet oasis of green for you to rest in during your stroll around the Yodoyabashi area (make a small donation at the main shrine building if you plan to stop here, though, as this is a local neighborhood shrine and not a typical tourist destination).

12. **Tsumura Betsuin Temple:** An important temple during the Edo Period (1600–1868), this temple (known as Kita Mido) was a central part of the thriving merchant culture of Osaka, and when Osaka's first grand north–south boulevard was built under the supervision of Mayor Seki Hajime, it was named Midosuji (Mido Boulevard) because this temple could be seen from the road. The current Tsumura Betsuin Temple is a modern structure, but when you ascend the staircase from Midosuji Blvd. its awesome scale will astonish you.

13. **Shibakawa Building:** This building was completed in 1927 and served as a private homemaking school until 1943. It has a classy, upscale design.

14. **Aishu Kindergarten:** Originally built in 1880 as one of the first kindergartens in Japan, this completely wooden, traditional Japanese building is, amazingly enough, still in use as a kindergarten today. Its tile roofs resemble those of a Buddhist temple complex.

15. **Tekijuku School of Dutch Learning:** Built 200 years ago, this old wooden structure is a true rarity in Japan. Formerly a merchant's house, it came into use as a private school of Dutch learning in 1838—at that time, Dutch knowledge was sometimes imported into Japan as a way of learning about European advances in medical science.

16. **Koraibashi Building:** This building was completed in 1912 in characteristic Meiji style, with red bricks (imported from England) outlined by white stone.

17. **Naniwa Church:** Constructed under the supervision of American architect William Merrel Vories, this gothic-style church is adorned with elegant stained-glass windows. It was completed in 1930.

18. **Semba Building:** Completed in 1925, the Semba Building was a combination office and residential complex, and it featured cutting-edge modern facilities (flushing toilets, mounted heaters, etc.) and design. Its architectural style and refreshing interior courtyard garden made it a breakthrough accomplishment at the time.

19. **Yuki Museum of Art:** This small art museum is a modern building displaying a selection of important works. Its initial collection was donated by Teiichi Yuki, a gourmet chef who also enjoyed Japanese tea ceremony (tea ceremony is one of the museum's themes).

20. **Naniwabashi Bridge:** An old stone bridge crossing over two rivers and the Nakanoshima riverine island, Naniwabashi is often called the "Lion Bridge" because of the pairs of gallant lion statues installed at both ends. Originally a wooden bridge,

it was later redesigned in the current manner to blend with the surrounding urban landscape and provide a suitable entrance to Nakanoshima Park.

21. **Kitahama Retro Building:** This building was completed in 1912 and originally owned by a stockbroker who eventually abandoned it. The current owner refurbished it at his own expense in 1997 to preserve its unique retro design.

22. **Osaka Securities Exchange Building:** This modern building, with its grand pillars and dome entrance leading to a glass-covered high-rise building, provides a fitting symbol for the Osaka Securities Exchange. As Japan's "merchant's capital" during the Edo Period (1600–1868), Osaka was home to the first futures exchange in world history, not far from this building's location.

23. **Arai Building:** Built using some of the most advanced architectural design features available at the time, this building was completed in 1922 under renowned architect Kozo Kawai. It was originally home to Hotoku Bank's Osaka branch.

24. **Koraibashi Nomura Building:** This is one of the loveliest buildings in Kitahama. It was completed in 1927, and its eye-catching Western design features smooth, flowing lines.

25. **Aoyama Building:** Built in 1921, this building was once the residence of a restaurant owner, and it now has a coffee shop on the first floor where you can enjoy charming, old-fashioned interior design. After World War II, the allied occupation considered using it as a headquarters building, but chose a different venue in the end.

26. **Fushimi Building:** Built as a hotel in 1923, the Fushimi Building now houses offices, an art gallery and a French restaurant.

27. **Sukunahikona Shrine:** A little hard to find, this tucked-away temple is best approached from between the buildings on the road on its south side. It enshrines the founder of Chinese medicine and a Japanese deity of medicine, and ever since the 1822 cholera outbreak in Osaka, people have come here to pray for good health and recovery from illness.

28. **Former Konishi Residence:** Easily one of the most impressive buildings in the Kitahama/Yodobashi area, this massive merchant's residence and storehouse complex is typical of wealthy Osaka merchants of times past. Leading Japanese medicine-makers flourished in this part of town during the nineteenth century, and Gisuke Konishi built this complex in 1903. Its black walls and imposing roof are symbols of power and wealth. The residence's merchant tradition continues to this day—it is currently used by a maker of synthetic adhesive.

29. **Ikoma Building:** Built in 1930 for a cost of ¥150,000 (a staggering sum at the time), this building once towered over the cityscape. It was originally owned by a watchmaker, which explains the clock tower on top and the building's unique grandfather-clock-themed design. The Ikoma Building has one of the most interesting retro building designs in Japan.

30. **Kishimoto Kawaramachi Residence:** This English-style residence was built for wealthy steel merchant Kichizaemon Kishimoto in 1931, and it stands out as a type of building not often encountered in Japan.

31. **The Entrepreneurial Museum of Challenge and Innovation:** This small museum gives an overview of famous entrepreneurs of Osaka, a city that has been home to some of the most innovative tradespeople and businesspeople in all of Japan's history, not to mention some of the most influential companies in the world today. Exhibits introduce 105 entrepreneurs, including the founders of Panasonic (formerly Matsushita) and Sharp, and even the inventor of instant ramen. Audio guides in four languages are available for free.

Tondabayashi Jinaimachi Map

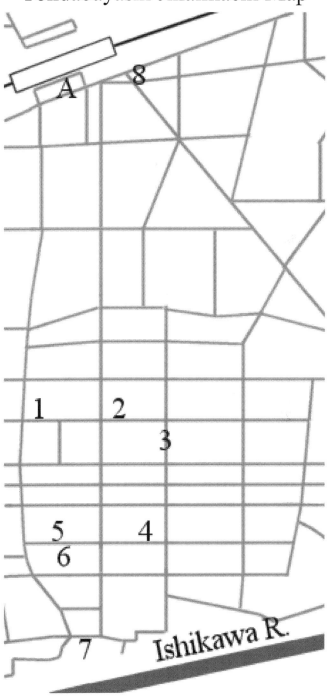

■ Tondabayashi Jinaimachi Map:

A. Tondabayashi Station (Kintetsu Nagano Line)

1. Jinaimachi terra

2. Jinaimachi Cultural Exchange Center

3. Jonomon-suji Street

4. Koshoji Betsuin Temple

5. Sugiyama Residence

6. Jinaimachi Center

7. Kastura Residence

8. Ongashi Tsukasa Katsura-ya

(See p. 131 for more details)

Sightseeing Destinations by Category

The following is a categorized list of the destinations in this guidebook with relevant page numbers and ratings, in order from highest to lowest rating (alphabetical for items with equal ratings). Note that ratings with an asterisk (*) by them are seasonal ratings, meaning they are rated based on seasonal events or conditions. The categories are Shrines and Temples; Museums; Historical Buildings and Sites; Parks and Nature; Shopping; Entertainment, Theatre and Sports; Districts; and Others (a few destinations are listed in more than one category). The area for each destination is listed using the following abbreviations:

M = Minami (p. 49)

K = Kita (p. 71)

C = Central Osaka City (p. 81)

CK = Osaka Castle Area / Kyobashi (p. 94)

TE = Tennoji / East Osaka City (p. 102)

WB = West Osaka City / Bay Area (p. 115)

S = South Osaka City (p. 124)

SP = Southern Osaka Prefecture (p. 129)

NP = Northern Osaka Prefecture (p. 147)

EP = Eastern Osaka Prefecture (p. 155)

Shrines and Temples

Destination	Area	Rating	Page
Hozanji Temple	EP	5	157
Sumiyoshi Grand Shrine	S	5	124

Eifukuji Temple (Prince Shotoku's Mausoleum)	SP	4	129
Hozenji Yokocho	M	4	52
Takidani Fudo Myo-oji Temple	SP	4	130
Imamiya-Ebisu Shrine	S	3*	125
Ishikiri-Tsurugiya Shrine	EP	3	155
Naniwa Yasaka Shrine	M	3	55
Nanshuji Temple	SP	3	134
Shitennoji Temple	TE	3	109
Daikoji Temple	NP	2	149
Domyoji Tenmangu Shrine and Domyoji Temple	SP	2	140
Fujiidera Temple	SP	2	140
Hiraoka Shrine	EP	2	156
Osaka Tenmangu Shrine	C	2	92
Sojiji Temple	NP	2	153
Hagi-no-tera Toko-in Temple	NP	1	150
Ikutama Shrine	TE	1	105
Isshinji Temple	TE	1	112
Karakuni Shrine	SP	1	141
Myokokuji Temple	SP	1	138
Ohatsu Tenjin (Tsuyuten Shrine)	K	1	78
Sanko Shrine	TE	1	106
Sayama Shrine	SP	1	134
Taiyuji Temple	K	1	79
Tamatsukuri Inari Shrine	TE	1	107
Tojiji Temple	TE	1	108

Museums

Destination	Area	Rating	Page
Osaka Museum of History	CK	5	96
The National Museum of Art, Osaka	C	4	83
Osaka Museum of Housing and Living	C	4	90
Peace Osaka (Osaka International Peace Center)	CK	4	97
Kishiwada Danjiri Hall	SP	3	143
The Museum of Oriental Ceramics, Osaka	C	3	84
National Museum of Ethnology	NP	3	152
Open-Air Museum of Old Japanese Farmhouses	NP	3	148
Sakai City Museum	SP	3	135
Fujita-tei Remains Park and Museum	CK	2	98
Osaka Maritime Museum	WB	2	118
Kamigata Ukiyoe Museum	M	1	59
Liberty Osaka (Osaka Human Rights Museum)	S	1	126
Osaka Science Museum	C	1	85

Historical Buildings and Sites

Destination	Area	Rating	Page
Osaka Castle Park	CK	5	94
Nakanoshima Historical Buildings and Bridges	C	4	81
Tondabayashi Jinaimachi Temple Town	SP	4	131
Tsutentaku and Shinsekai	TE	4	103
Kishiwada Castle	SP	3	142

Kitahama/Yodoyabashi Historical Buildings	C	3	86
Open-Air Museum of Old Japanese Farmhouses	NP	3	148
Mozu Tumulus Cluster	SP	2	136
Osaka Shinkabukiza	M	2	58
Naniwa Palace Historical Park	CK	1	100
Old Sakai Lighthouse	SP	1	139

Parks and Nature

Destination	Area	Rating	Page
Minoh Park	NP	5	147
Osaka Castle Park	CK	5	94
Banpaku Memorial Park	NP	4	150
Mount Ikoma Summit	EP	158	157
Shimo-Akasaka Terraced Rice Fields	SP	3	133
Fujita-tei Remains Park and Museum	CK	2	98
Mozu Tumulus Cluster	SP	2	136
Tsurumi Ryokuchi Park	TE	2	112
Utsubo Park	C	2	88
Hamadera Park	SP	1	137
Mount Tempozan	WB	1	121
Nagai Park	S	1	127
Nakanoshima Park	C	1	85
Naniwa Palace Historical Park	CK	1	100
Yodogawa Lagoons / Shirokita Park	TE	1	113

Shopping

Destination	Area	Rating	Page
Sennichimae Doguyasuji Shopping Arcade	M	5	60
Shinsaibashi Shopping Arcade	M	5	68
Umeda / Osaka Station Area	K	5	71
Amemura	M	4	66
Den Den Town	M	4	62
Namba Parks	M	4	53
Namba Underground Shopping	M	4	54
Shinbashi Intersection	M	4	69
Chayamachi	K	3	73
Kuromon Market	M	3	64
HEP FIVE and HEP NAVIO	K	3	75
Rinku Town	SP	3	144
Takashimaya Department Store	M	3	56
Tenjinbashisuji Shopping Arcade	C	3	91
Crysta Nagahori	M	2	70
Marui	M	2	57
OCAT	M	2	57
The Asia & Pacific Trade Center (ATC)	WB	1	119
Semba Center Building	C	1	90

Entertainment, Theatre and Sports

Destination	Area	Rating	Page
Osaka Aquarium Kaiyukan	WB	5	115
Universal Studios Japan	WB	5	116
National Bunraku Theatre	M	4	63

Osaka Prefectural Gymnasium (Sumo)	M	4*	55
ddd gallery	M	3	66
HEP FIVE and HEP NAVIO	K	3	75
Rinku Town	SP	3	144
Tempozan Giant Ferris Wheel and Tempozan Marketplace	WB	3	117
Umeda Joypolis	K	3	76
Expo '70 Commemorative Stadium (Gamba Osaka Soccer Stadium)	NP	2	153
Kyocera Dome Osaka	WB	2	122
Namba Grand Kagetsu Theatre	M	2	64
Osaka Shinkabukiza	M	2	58
Yamamoto Noh Theatre	C	2	89

Districts

Destination	Area	Rating	Page
Dotombori and Ebisubashi	M	5	49
Sennichimae Doguyasuji Shopping Arcade	M	5	60
Umeda / Osaka Station Area	K	5	71
Amemura	M	4	66
Den Den Town	M	4	62
Tondabayashi Jinaimachi Temple Town	SP	4	131
Tsutentaku and Shinsekai	TE	4	103
Chayamachi	K	3	73
Hankyu Higashidori	K	3	74
Kita-Horie and Minami-Horie	M	3	67
Tenjinbashisuji Shopping Arcade	C	3	91

Tsuruhashi	TE	3	105
Fukushima	K	2	76
Juso	K	2	77
Kitashinchi	WB	2	77
Kujo Neighborhood	K	2	122
Tennoji/Abenobashi	TE	2	110
Kyobashi	CK	1	99
Osaka Business Park	CK	1	101
Shin-Osaka	K	1	79

Others

Destination	Area	Rating	Page
Umeda Sky Building	K	5	72
Aqua Bus Tours	M/C/CK	4	51
Spa World	TE	4	102
Kuromon Market	M	3	64
Santa Maria Bay Cruise	WB	2	119
Cosmo Tower	WB	1	120
Kansai International Airport	SP	1	145
Minatomachi River Place	M	1	60

15886063R00115

Made in the USA
Lexington, KY
22 June 2012